ANCIENT MYSTIC

ORIENTAL MASONRY

Its teachings, Rules, Laws and Present Usages
which govern the Order at the present day.

"TRUE MASONRY AND THE UNIVERSAL BROTHER-
HOOD OF MAN ARE ONE."

BY DR. R. SWINBURNE CLYMER

*Author of "The Rosicrucians: their Teachings;" The
Philosophy of Fire," etc.*

Published by
The Philosophical Publishing Co.
Allentown, Pa.

DEDICATION

To Henry J. Barton, M. D., The American Deputy, Thos. Benj. OmiCole and Prof. A. F. Davies, of far off Africa, to those Masonic Brethren who have helped to make this work possible, to that Fraternity who has been the Life of the work in the past as at present, and above all, to that one who has been the Guiding Star of my work, is this book Lovingly Dedicated.

R. SWINBURNE CLYMER

INTRODUCTORY.

In placing the present work before the public I have no apology whatever to offer, and this for several reasons. First, because I have been ordered to prepare it, and Second, because much of what I herein give is not new, for the simple reason that there can be nothing new in Masonry. True, many a thing, especially what concerns Mystic Masonry, has not been given to a profane people, but this is not to say that it is new, for it is not.

I know that the present work will stand unchallenged as to the Truths it contains, and this for the reason that *I quote from the highest Masonic authorities in the world,* and that which concerns Mystic Masonry comes *direct from him who knows and who has no superior in this work.*

I also *know* that I will not be accused of stealing, for the very good reason that I give credit for every single quotation, unless it was changed. With these facts before me I can feel well satisfied to let it go forward.

There are several reasons why this book should go before the people, and especially before Masons themselves. Too little is known by my Brother Masons concerning that Order to which they have the honor to belong, but which some of them do not honor and the

1a

present work, prepared from the highest authorities, will give them some idea of what the underlying principle of their teachings is.

It has also become necessary to let the world know that Mystic Masonry exists and has existed for many years, although not always under that name. Not much can be said concerning the Order, for the reason that even its degrees may not become known to a profane world. Craft Masons can learn all they desire concerning it, provided they are willing to pay the price, not in current coin, but in their duty and in work.

Initiation is not what it is generally supposed to be. All Masons know what Ceremonial Initiation is, but this is simply the outward symbol of the *inner* work. A Mason who has the three degrees may think that he has all that can be had, but little does he know of that *inner* work, that Grand and Supreme Initiation which is possible for those who truly desire it.

Thousands of good men take the letter for the Spirit and it is in doing this where the misunderstanding begins. Nothing new can come to Masonry, but there is a world of Truth in Masonry that the vast majority know nothing whatever about, and it is for this reason that the present work is placed before the public and especially before all Brother Masons, and it is sent forth in such a manner that it cannot be denied, for as stated before, it is from *the highest authorities among all Masons.*

As regard to the *true* Initiation, I would quote from

the work of that Master Mason, Dr. J. D. Buck, in which he says:

"Initiation and Regeneration are synonymous terms."

"The Ritual of Freemasonry is based on this natural law, and the ceremony of initiation illustrates, at every step, this principle, and if the result attained is a possession rather than a regeneration, in the great majority of cases, the principle remains none the less true. The mere inculcation of moral principles, or lessons in ethics, and their symbolic illustration and dramatic representation, are by no means in vain. These appeal to the conscience and moral sense in every man, and no man has ever been made worse by the Lessons of the Lodge. By these 'rites and benefits,' the Freemason is, above all men, in our so-called Modern Civilization, the nearest to the Ancient Wisdom. He has possession of the territory in which lie concealed the Crown Jewels of Wisdom. He may content himself, if he will, *by merely turning over the sod and gathering only a crop of husks or stubble.* He may dig deeper and find not only the Keystone of the Arch, the Ark of the Covenant, the Scroll or the Law, but, using the Spirit concealed in the wings of the Cherubim, he may rise untrammeled by the rubbish of the temple, and, meeting Elohim face to face, learn also to say *'I am that I am!'* Does this read like a rhapsody, and are the Landmarks, traditions, and glyphics of Freemasonry nothing more?"

And again: "The Universal Science and the Sublime Philosophy, once taught in the Greater Mysteries of Egypt, Chaldea, Persia, and India, and among many other nations of antiquity, is a dead letter in modern Freemasonry. The intelligent Mason, however, should be the *last* person in the world to deny that such Wisdom once existed, for the simple reason the whole superstructure of. Masonry is built *upon* the traditions of its existence, and its ritual serves as its living monument. Proficiency in the preceding degree is everywhere made a reason for advancement in Masonry. This proficiency is made to consist in the ability of the candidate to repeat word for word, certain rituals and obligations already passed, the meaning and explanations of which constitute the lectures in the various degrees. The usage at this point, in the United States at least, serves rather to secure the rights and benefits of the Lodge to those entitled to them, and to withhold them from others, than to advance the candidate in *real* Knowledge.''

For this very reason the present work is placed before all those who would know. Mystic Masonry also has its Rituals and its laws, but it makes the Spirit of *more* value than the letter and *will* teach its candidates the Spirit as well as the letter, for in its higher degrees the man must bring *out* that which is *in* him if he desires to advance. In this way the *real* Initiation does not only become a possibility but a *fact* and none can advance unless they do the work. Besides this, Mystic Masonry *does* what Craft Masonry *should* do— it binds its men into one Universal Brotherhood in which they *must* treat each other as brothers if they desire to remain in the Order. This is not a dream, but a *reality*.

Says Dr. Buck again: "We do not know a thing because we are *told* so. Let the gods shout the Truth of all ages into the ears of a fool forever, and still forever the fool would be joined to his folly. *Here lies the conception and the principal of all Initiations.* It is knowledge *unfolded by degrees in an orderly, systematic manner, step by step, as the capacity to apprehend opens in the Neophyte.* The result is not a possession, but a *growth,* an *evolution.* Knowledge is not a mere sum in addition; something added to something that already exists; but rather such a progressive change or *transformation* of the original structure as to make it, at every step, a New Being. Real Knowledge, or the growth of Wisdom *in* man, is an Eternal Becoming; a progressive transformation into the likeness of the Supernal Goodness and the Supreme Power."

In a work of this nature, not too much can be said as regard the Supreme Initiation, and those who may be *truly* interested I would refer to "The Rosicrucians; their Teachings," and to "The Philosophy of Fire," both of which contain Chapters on the *true* Initiation.

Ninety-nine Masons out of every hundred would laugh at the Occult Science, and yet, were it not for the Occult Fraternities, Masonry could never have existed. The Secret Doctrine was the universally diffused religion of the Ancient and prehistoric world. Proof of its diffusion, authentic records of its history, a complete chain of documents, showing its character and presence in every land, together with the teaching of all its great Adepts, exist to this day in the secret crypts of libraries belonging to the Occult Fraternities. The Rosicrucian Fraternity, more than any other, is to be thanked for keeping the Secret and Sacred writings intact. Although the Individual members of this Fraternity have been persecuted in many lands and during all centuries, the Order or Fraternity, as such, has never been persecuted, nor has there been any interruption. This Fraternity, therefore, has been able to continue, without interruption, the teachings of the Secret Doctrine and Ancient Mysteries. No matter what the Order, whether Masonry or Mystic Masonry, no matter the name, it has always been found that Rosicrucians had the work in hand. History proves this, it cannot be successfully denied, and none but those who are ignorant try to deny it.

Every Soul must "work out its own Salvation." Salvation by faith and the vicarious atonement were *not* taught, as now interpreted, by Jesus, nor are these doctrines taught in the exoteric Scriptures. They are later and ignorant perversions of the *original* doctrines. In the Early Church, as in the Secret Doctrine, there was not one Christ for the whole world, but a *potential* Christ *in* every man. Theologians first made a fetish of the Impersonal, Omnipresent Divinity; and then tore the *Christos* from the hearts of all humanity in order to deify Jesus; that they might have a God made peculiarly their own. Masonry does *not* teach Salvation by Faith nor the Vicarious atonement. Go through its degrees, study the History as taught by its greatest Masters, and you·cannot find that it teaches this Doctrine. Boldly do I claim that this doctrine does *not* make Christians, but it *does* make criminals. The reason for this is plain. All the Ancient Mysteries had the *true* Doctrine, and so had the early Christians. Masonry, *before it was contaminated by the disciples of Loyala—the Jesuits—* had it also. It is for Masons to bring out the good and the true from the rubbish.

Says Bro. Buck again: "Humanity *in toto* is the only Personal God; the *Christos* is the realization, or perfection of this Divine *Persona,* in Individual conscious experience. When this perfection is realized, the state is called *Christos,* with the Greeks, and *Buddha* with the Hindoos. 'Be ye perfect, even as your Father in Heaven is Perfect.'

Then, my brother, if Christ and Buddha are *one* and the *same, why* condemn you those that follow the *Buddha?* Know you not that they who Follow the *Buddha* follow the same *Christ* as you under but another name?

"We have brought the same selfishness into our religion that we indulge in regard to our other possessions, such as wife and children, and houses and land, and country; and the same partisan spirit as in our politics, and this more than anything else appears to justify selfishness in general, militates against the Brotherhood of man, and prevents the founding of the 'Great Republic, composed of many Nations and all people.' This idea of Universal Brotherhood, which was a cardinal doctrine in the Ancient Mysteries—as it is involved in the first postulate of the Secret Doctrine, and openly declared in the third; and which is equally given the very first rank in (true) Masonry—is the logical deduction from our idea of Divinity, and of the essential nature and meaning of *Christos.*"

In Mystic Masonry this idea of the Universal Brotherhood of Man is one of the Supreme Laws and a Cardinal Principle. Before the Candidate can start out in even the first degree of Mystic Oriental Masonry he must subscribe to the Rules of a Universal Brotherhood, and this is not a dead letter, for the Secret Code will see to it that he not only Obligates to treat all other members of the Order as Brothers, but that *he will do it.* There is no exception to this rule, all alike must obey it or pay the natural penalty. There can be no exception to this rule. Brother for Brother and *not* Brother against Brother. We live or die together.

"Masonry, nor Mystic Masonry, does not preach a new religion, it but reiterates the New Commandment announced by Jesus, which was also announced by every great reformer or religion since history began. Drop the theological barnacles from the Religion of Jesus, as taught by Him, and by the Essenes and Gnostics of the first centuries, and it becomes (Mystic) Masonry. Masonry, in its purity, derived as it is from the old Kabalah as a part of the Great Universal Wisdom Religion of the remotest Antiquity, stands squarely for the Unqualified and Universal Brotherhood of Man, in all times and in every age. To Christianize Masonry, or to narrow it to the sectarian bonds of any Creed, is not only to dwarf and belittle it, but must inevitably result, as among warring sects, has always resulted with religion, in setting brother against brother, and Lodge against Lodge.''

Mystic Masonry can recognize neither color nor creed, and in that lies its safety and through this will it gradually bring about the Universal Brotherhood of Man. It not only teaches this but all those who belong to it *must* practice it. Is there not a wave of Brotherhood sweeping over every land? Do not the reports show that this work is spreading as never before? What then is to prevent it from growing larger and larger until the majority will subscribe to Brotherhood? The fiat is cast, the results are sure.

''So long as the lower mind is held in bondage by desire, man can not seek or discern the Good or the True. He inquires, 'What is good *for me?*' Freed from Desire, or the personal bias, he inquires after and seeks for that which is good or true *in itself*. When this condition is reached and habitually maintained, the square is said to be inclosed in the triangle. The lower nature is said to be at one with the Divine, or Spiritual Soul. Man's knowledge and power are no longer confined to, or circumscribed by, the lower plane, or the physical body; but, transcending these by Regeneration (self-conquest), and becoming perfect in Humanity, man attains Divinity. This is the meaning, aim, and consummation of Human Evolution; and this Philosophy defines the one-only process by which it may be attained.

''The Perfect Man is Christ: and Christ is God.

This is the birth-right and destiny of every human
soul. It was taught in all the Greater Mysteries of
Antiquity, but the Exoteric creeds of Christiandom derived from the parables and allegories in which this
doctrine was concealed from the ignorant and the profane, have accorded this Supreme Consummation to
Jesus alone, and made it obscure or impossible for all
the rest of humanity. In place of this, the grandest
doctrine ever revealed to man, theologians have set up
Salvation by Faith in a man-made Creed, and the
Authority of the Church to 'bind or lose on Earth or
in Heaven.' Law is annulled, Justice dethroned,
Merit ignored, Effort discouraged, and Sectarianism,
Atheism, and Materialism are the results.

All real Initiation is an *internal,* not an external
process. The outer ceremony is dead and useful only
so far as it symbolizes and illustrates, and thereby
makes clear the inward change. To transform means
to *regenerate,* and this comes by trial, by effort, by
self-conquest, by sorrow, disappointment, *failure,* and
a daily renewal of the conflict. It is thus man must
'work out his own salvation.' The consummation of
initiation is the finding of the *Christos.*"

The problem of genuine Initiation, or training in
occultism, consists in placing all the operations of the
body under the dominion of the Will. In freeing the
Ego from the dominion of the appetites, passions, and
the whole lower nature. The idea is not to despise the
body, but to purify or *transmute* it. Not to destroy
the appetites, but to elevate and control them absolutely, and this is known in Alchemy as the *transmuta-*

tion. This mastery of the lower nature does not change the Key of the physical nature as such; but subordinates it to that of a Higher plane. Without this subordination, the clamorous lower animal nature drowns out all higher vibrations; as if in an orchestra, the bass-viols and the drums only could be heard; and noise rather than harmony, results. Hence the saying: "He that conquers *himself* is greater than he who taketh a city."

Says Dr. Buck: "While every *true* Mason is the most loyal of men to every office of woman, as Mother, Sister, Daughter and Wife; as Companion, Friend, and Inspirer of man, he would have been trammeled by her presence in the Lodge, and she would have received *no* benefit by being admitted. When, however, the days of Ritualism alone are ended, when from the one duty of guarding the altars and lighting the camp-fires, Masonry resumes its prerogative as Teacher and Enlightener of mankind, and the Philosophy of Nature and of Life are unfolded in its Schools and Colleges as with the Magi of old, and when with no fear of persecution from time-serving Potentate or Creed-ridden Priest, the Light may shine for all, then will the doors of *real* Initiation be as open to woman as to man, as was the case in the schools of Pythagoras as shown by Iamlichus. The Ancient Wisdom concerned itself largely with the Souls of men, and undertook to elevate the earthly life by purifying the Soul and exalting its Ideals. It teaches that souls are Sexless, and that the sex of the body is an incident of gestation.

"No civilization known to man has ever risen to any great heights, or long maintained its supremacy, that debased woman. Indeed, the Secret Doctrine demonstrates with unmistakable clearness that sexual debasement in *any* form is the highway to degeneracy and destruction of both man and woman; and of Nations quite as certainly as of individuals."

'When Brother Buck penned the above, he could not have been aware of the fact that the Rosicrucian Fraternity accepted women on an equal footing as men in all its degrees. It is for this very reason that the Rosicrucian Fraternity has been able to go unmolested, when other orders were persecuted. It is also for this same reason that the Catholic Church has been able to bring to its fold almost as many men and women as nearly all other churches combined. They recognize the Mother principle in Deity and know that man and woman, the twain are *one.*

Mystic Masonry recognizes this same principle and while it cannot admit women to its ceremonial Initiation, provisions are made whereby they can reach as high as can men. This is a wise plan, a plan founded by those who *know* and who know *why the* Rosicrucian Fraternity is as strong and as *silent* as it is.

While Mary of Magdalia could not be a disciple of Jesus, and could not travel with Him and His other disciples, yet, she could be taught in secret by Him and when all others, his most trusted disciples swore that they did not know him, Mary, *the woman,* did not fear to stand by Him. *Let Mystic Masons remember.*

Allentown, Pa.   THE AUTHOR.
Thanksgiving, 1906

DEGREES OF THE

MYSTIC ORIENTAL RITE

Grand Master of the Secret Manuscript.

It came to pass when the temple was completed that Solomon hesitated to dedicate it for two reasons:

First. On account of the death of Hiram Abiff.

Second. On account of the fact that with the death of the Widow's Son, the Master's Word and the secret manner of using it had been lost. Therefore, Solomon in his extremity called a secret council at low-twelve in the secret crypt under the Sanctum Sanctorum.

This secret Council consisted of Solomon, King of Israel, Hiram, King of Tyre, Zadok, the High Priest, Benaiah, Captain of the Guards.

After Solomon had deplored the loss of Hiram Abiff, and with him the Master's Word and the Secret manner of using it, Hiram, King of Tyre, arose and reminded King Solomon that Nathan, the Prophet, was still alive and might render some assistance in his present calamity. Solomon, therefore, ordered Benaiah, Captain of the Guards, to search out and bring before him Nathan, the Prophet.

2

Benaiah, having ascertained that Nathan the Prophet was at the house of Abiathar, a former High Priest under King David, repaired to the place, but found that Nathan had died of old age but a very short time before his arrival; he thereupon set about to return and discovering a stranger wandering near the Secret Crypt, he thereupon took him into his custody and brought him before the Secret Council. The stranger proved to be Abdemon, a very wise man and a subject of Hiram, King of Tyre. Upon examination it was found that he had been initiated as an Entered Apprentice, Passed to the degree of a Fellow Craft, and raised to the Sublime Degree of a Master Mason by Seisan, a Scribe, who had journeyed into the country of the Tyrians, so that the Secrets of Masonry preceded Hiram, King of Tyre, into his own Dominions.

Abdemon, being a Master Mason, and being recognized as a very learned and crafty man by King Hiram, was at length admitted to the Secret Council after giving into the hands of King Solomon a Manuscript that had been given to him in a wonderful and mysterious manner by an Egyptian during the time he was held in confinement by the Secret Council. Solomon was so pleased with the manuscript that he then and there admitted Abdemon as a member of the Secret Council, which was then sitting. Abdemon in his turn felt himself so highly honored that he begged leave and received permission to journey into the land of Egypt and be initiated into the secrets of the Initiates of the Great Pyramid, and in turn promised to journey back into the land of the Israelites and disclose to the Secret Council what he had learned. Abdemon was successful in his efforts and the following degrees were instituted to preserve the knowledge which Abdemon gained in the land of Egypt and his journey and initiation in the Great Stone Pyramid.

Second. "The King's Pioneer."

Third. "Degree of Master of the Secret Cavern."

After resting for three days at the well of Beersheba, Ameni, the Singer, the Horoscopus and Abdemon, under the escort of the King's Pioneer, journeyed by easy stages to Mount Serbal, where the parties took refuge in a natural cave where Abdemon received his final instructions before his initiation into the Degree of the Pyramid

During the course of the journey Ameni disclosed many hidden Mysteries to Abdemon concerning initiation and why it was impossible to make these disclosures to the multitude in general.

Among the things which Ameni communcated to Abdemon on their journey, the following is the most important, for said he:

"Before appearing on earth, man lived in a spiritual world, similar to the one in which he lives on leaving the earth. Each awaits his turn in this world to appear on earth, an appearance necessary, a life of trials none can escape.

"The life anterior, which we have all passed through, was, so to speak, a life of nothingness, of childbirth, of happiness like that which we enjoy on our exit from the earth; but this happiness cannot be comprehended,

because it is not accompanied with sensations to prove
its sweet reality, therefore God has deemed fit that we
should pass through these successive lives, the first, on
the globes of which I speak to you—a life unknown,
of beatitude, devoid of sensation—the second, the one
you enjoy, a life of action, sensation—a painful life
placed between the two, to demonstrate through its
contrast the sweetness of the third—the life of good
and evil, without which we should not be able to ap-
preciate the happy state reserved for us.

"That the Soul is an emanation of Deity, and in its
original essence is all purity, truth, and wisdom, is an
axiom which the disembodied learn, when the powers
of memory are sufficiently awakened to perceive the
states of existence anterior to mortal birth. In the
Paradises of Purity and Love, Souls spring up like
blossoms, in the all Father's garden on Immortal
beauty. It is the tendency of the Divine nature whose
chief attributes are Love and Wisdom, Heat and
Light, to repeat itself eternally, and mirror forth its
own perfection in scintillations from *itself*. These
sparks of heavenly *fire* become Souls, and as the effect
must share in the nature of the cause, the *fire* which
warms into life, also illuminates into Light, hence the
Soul emanations from the Divine are all Love and
Heat, whilst the illumination of Light, which streams
ever from the great Central Sun of Being, irradiates
all Souls with corresponding beams of Light. Born of
Love which corresponds to Divine Heat and Warmth,
and irradiated with Light, which is Divine Wisdom
and Truth, the first and most powerful Souls repeated

the action of the Supreme Originator, gave off emina-
tions from their own being, some higher, some lower,
the highest tending upward into Spiritual essences,
the lowest forming particled matter. These denser
emanations, following out the creative law, aggregated
into Suns, Satellites, Worlds, and each repeating the
Story of Creation. Suns gave birth to Systems, and
every member of a system became a theatre of sub-
ordinate states of Spiritual or material existence.

"Earths that have attained to the capacity to support organic life, necessarily attract it. Earths demand it, Heaven supplies it. From whence? *As the
earths groan for the lordship of superior beings to rule
over them, the Spirits in the distant Edens, hear the
whispers of the tempting Serpent, the animal principle, the urgent intellect, which appealing to the blest
Souls in their distant paradises, fill them with inde-
scribable longings for change, for broader vistas of
knowledge, for mightier powers; they would be as the
gods, and know good and evil; and in this urgent appeal of the earths for man, and this involuntary yearn-
ing of the Spirit for intellectual knowledge, the union
is effected between the two, and the spirit becomes pre-
cipitated into the realms of matter to undergo a
pilgrimage through the probationary states of earth,
and only to regain paradise again by the fulfillment of
that pilgrimage.*"

The names of the other four degrees it is not even
lawful for me to state in a public manner, but sufficient
for me it is to say that the manner and order of the
officers of the Great Pyramid was as follows:

2a

"The Chief or Singer, who carries an instrument symbolical of music, and two books of Hermes, one of them containing the hymns of the gods, and the other the list of the kings. After him comes the Horoscopist, observer of the seasons, carrying a palm-branch and a time-piece symbolic of Astrology. He has to know by heart the four books of Hermes, which treat of Astrology: the first of which treats of the order of the planets, the second of the rising and setting of the Sun and Moon, and third and fourth of their movements in their orbits, and the aspects of the stars. Then comes the Sacred writer, having some ...., and in his hands a book, an ink-bottle, and a reed for writing, according to the manner of the Priests. This officer has to understand the language of the hieroglyphics, the description of the universe, the courses of the sun, moon, and planets, the divisions of Egypt into thirty-six districts, the course of the Nile, the Sacred ornaments, the Holy places, etc. Then comes the stole bearer, who carries the gauge of Justice, or measure of the Nile, and a Chalice for libations, together with ten volumes containing the sacrifices, the hymns, the prayers, the offerings, and ceremonies of the feasts. Finally appears the Prophet, carrying in his bosom, but exposed, a pitcher. He is followed by those who carry the bread, as at the marriage of Cana. This Prophet, in his position as Keeper of the Mysteries, must know by heart the ten volumes which treat of the Laws, of the gods, and of all the disciples of the Priests, etc., which are outside of the forty-two volumes. Thirty-six are known by

these persons, and the other six, treating of medicine,
of the construction of the human frame, of sickness,
of medicaments, and of surgical instruments, belong
to the postophores.

MYSTIC MASONRY

1. *Mystic Masonry is not only the key to the religion taught to all men in all ages from the very beginning of conscious life up to the present, but it holds the keys to these religious and is, in fact, the very repository of religion itself. Its degrees give this secret to its initiates as no religion nor any other order can. It has for its base the existence of God and the immortality of the soul. It recognizes man as the living temple of God, that temple which was built without sound of hammer or any noise whatever. It recognizes the Christos (Christ) as the living principle of the soul of man and without which no one can be immortal. It has for its object the uniting of mankind into a Universal Brotherhood, the exercise of benevolence; the practice of the arts; the practice of virtue and the study of both Nature and God as He is.*

2. The language used may seem strong, but we who know the work in these degrees must be the ones to judge as to what they are and what they contain. The Degrees, starting with the First up to the eleventh, teach all there is of Religion, they *give the key to religion itself.*

3. The Ancient and Mystic Oriental· Rite is Universal, and is open to every Master Mason who believes in the Fatherhood of God and the Universal Brotherhood of all Men. The other qualification necessary of the Neophyte is that he shall be honorable and upright in his dealings.

4. The cradle of the Symbolism used in all Masonry is placed by many of the best authorities in that country which they believe was first inhabited, *i. e.*, the plateau of Tartary, and from there transmitted to this generation by the sages of India, Persia, Ethiopia, and Egypt. We *are not indebted to either ancient Egypt for either Religion or Masonry, but to America.*

5. It is a fact that at Memphis, Egypt, in the Pyramids, under the guidance of the Kings, the Mystic Rites of Masonry were worked many thousands of years ago, but at that time Egypt and the continent of *America were one and the same.*

6. "In America, re-discovered in the fifteenth century and re-populated in the seventeenth, was re-covered Egypt and the promised land, or the land of the constellation of the Eagle."*

7. "No matter how numerous or complicated the works of a lock may be, if but the right key be applied. The Great Pyramid *proves to be the long-sought key to the mysteries at once of Mythology and of the great world religions.* Especially interesting is it to Americans in this year of the Columbian celebration of the four hundredth anniversary of the *re-*discovery of America, to see it demonstrated that the cosmic terrors

Parsons, "New Light from the Great Pyramid."

interwoven with the very warp and woof of all sacred literature, Christian and pagan, refer to occurrences as literally true as the earthquake of Lisbon, these stupendous events being connected primarily with a great destruction and recovery of equilibrium in the solar system;* and secondly with the consequent wrecking of the continent of America when the globe became involved in the consequences of the disorder of the skies. America (known to the Mystic as Atlantis), when this ruin befel, *was the seat of the greatest empire that has ever existed, and its irresistible armies were terrorizing all Europe and Asia.*

8. "Study of the American constellations Scorpio, Sagittarius, and Capricornus, reveals the immemorial antiquity of the name of America, and the significance of the arms of the United States. The fact once recognized that it is impossible to separate the Eagle from America—the "Land shadowed with wings" of Isaiah, over which accordingly appear two grand eagles, the red swan flying down the milky way, and the winged steeds, Yegasus, and Equelus, all the wings known to astronomy—without taking the Bear from Russia, Perseus from Persia, and a flood of light is poured upon the history and mythology; and where heretofore much has been vague and inscrutable, now we are able at least, to see men, as trees, walking.

9. "When, following the course of the constellations, those immovably and perpetually fastened upon America are reached, it will appear that, while all that is sublime in the historic past centers upon Egypt, *all that is sublime in the prehistoric past centers upon*

*See Philosophy of Fire

America (Atlantis); and as the curtain which has hitherto concealed the prehistoric connection between the peoples of ancient Egypt and of America, is lifted, it will be seen that, the people of the Eagle on the Nile being descended from the original people of the Eagle on this Continent, the twain are one, and that prehistoric America was the Original Egypt or Eagleland, prior to the mighty dispensation* in the days of Peleg, when the earth was divided, and the great globe itself was nearly rent asunder." **

10 Says Agassiz: "First born among continents, America has been falsely denominated the New World. Hers was the first dry land lifted out of the Waters, hers was the first shore washed by the ocean that enveloped all the earth besides; and while Europe was represented only by islands rising here and there above the sea, America (Atlantis) already stretched in an unbroken line of land from Nova Scotia to the far West."

11. "America was evidently peopled from the old continent, because there were only eight persons saved at the Deluge; the principal part of their posterity, during the whole of the first century after that event, occupied the very center of Asia. Some say that America was peopled by the Carthagenians who possessed the Cape Verd Islands, which are only three weeks sail from that continent. Their ships, having women and children on board, might miss the intended Islands, before the invention of the compass;

*See Philosophy of Fire
**Parsons, "New Light from the Great Pyramid."

and if so, they would inevitably be driven by the Trade Winds to the coast of America. Others, judging from the similarity of some religious rites, have conjectured that it was peopled by the Ten Tribes at the dispersion of Israel. Some think it received its population from China or Japan; others that it was colonized by some wandering tribes of Japheth, who penetrated into the trackless regions of North America by the straits of Asian. Some have been bold enough to assert that America *was not inundated at the Deluge, and that, consequently, the aborigines were Antediluvians, and the most ancient people on earth, (which last assertion is correct).* Others suppose that there were few individuals preserved on this vast continent at the Deluge, that it might be without difficulty repeopled. And we are told, "That America was peopled after the Deluge, at the same time as it were (communibus aliis), with other parts of the earth equidistant from the spot whereon the Ark is acknowledged to have grounded. For *the grand division of the Eastern and Western Hemispheres through the natural effect of causes operating from the Deluge, did not take place till about half a century after that event;* and thus a subject that has uniformly puzzled the most learned historians and philosophers, and given ground for the most elaborate dissertations, namely, the manner by which America was peopled, appears to be made simple and easy, as are all those questions that are submitted to the ordeal of truth, the infallable attestations of Holy Writ. Robertson supposes the Americans to have derived their original from the Asiatics; and supports his conjecture by some ancient traditions amongst the Mexicans, which ascribe their primitive population to a horde from a remote country to the northwest; whose gradual progress from the northern coast, where they landed, to the interior provinces, is distinctly traced. And, in the infancy of Christianity, Mexico is said to have been in a more advanced state of civilization than Denmark, Sweden, and Russia.

12. From what people soever Americans descended, or in whatever manner that vast continent was originally furnished with human beings; it is certain that the first inhabitants brought *with* them a system of Mysteries which they applied to the purposes of Religious Worship, and though this system, in process of time, was almost entirely lost amongst the scattered tribes which led an erratic life in its deepest wilds, yet *many* of the Truths on which it was founded, were preserved in a deteriorated form, by the two great nations which had planted themselves on each side of the Isthmus of Panama.'' *

13. "'The people who erected the obelisks in Egypt and covered them with hieroglyphics, who wrapped mummies, embalming them with the greatest care, knew no more about the pyramid builders than we do to-day. These majestic, voiceless sentinels—the pyramids—with heads uncovered and lifted heavenward, stood there on the broad plain silent and dumb, with no one to explain their origin, *when Egyptian ciliilization began.* **

---

* Oliver, "History of "Initiation."
** Jurden.

14. Of this there can be no doubt. The Pyramids were built by Atlantians long centuries before Egypt was a civilized country. Why then were they built in Egypt instead of on some part of what is now America? *Because Egypt was then the center of the earth and the Atlantians with their vast knowledge sought the center, for that will stand as long as time.*

15. That no one knew *why* the Pyramids were built is a wrong conclusion for we, of the Mystic Order of Masonry, *know* that they were built for no other purpose than for Supreme Initiation, for it must be remembered that there have ever been two Religions founded on the one Principle. The one for The Priests and the other for the People. Not only does the Initiation in Mystic Oriental Masonry explain the *very* foundation of All Religions, but it gives the Key to the Pyramids and unlocks the doors of the same.

16. The shape of the Pyramid itself has one of the deepest meanings to the Initiates. A Pyramid, the triangular form of it, *signifies fire,* and the cubical form the earth visited by fire. Fire in turn signifies *Love, God,* the *Fatherhood* of God. Could the Initiates have built a more lasting monument to the fact that they, above all others, *knew* God as but few men *know* Him at the present day?

17. "The Egyptian Pyramids excite in us the feeling of the sublime, not only on account of their spacial vastness, but also of their great age, we feel ourselves dwarfed to insignificance in their presence, and yet revel in the pleasure of contemplating them. In the presence of such a monument of ancient times, which

has outlived the knowledge of itself, we stand as sense-
less and stupid as the brute in the presence of the
action of man, or as a man before something written
in an old cipher of his own, the key to which he has
forgotten. For who will believe that those who at
incalculable cost set in action the human powers of
many thousands for many years in order to construct
the Pyramids, which have already existed for thousands of years, could have had in view the short span
of their own life, too short to let them see the finishing
of the construction, or even the ostensible end which
the ignorance of the many required them to allege?
Clearly, their *real* end was to speak to their latest descendants, to put themselves in communication with
these, and so to establish the unity on the *consciousness of humanity.*" *

18. "It is further certain that so much science, labor,
and treasure as were required for erecting so extraordinary and gigantic a structure would not have been
expended by men so skillful and ingenious as its
builders *were*, without an end in view fully commen-
surate, in their own minds, with the magnitude of the
project. Hence, if astronomy shows that the Great
Pyramid was planned with reference to a relation
between Alcyone and the Pleiades and some pole star
(possibly Alpha Draconis), obviously that relation
must have been of the highest importance in the cosmo-
logical systems of the builders—the veritable key, perhaps, to all the Wisdom of antiquity.

* Schopenhauser.

19. "To those ancient sages, the cosmos was literally uni-verse, or a revolution around one center. Their doctrines of the Unity of Nature, now confirmed by Spectrum Analysis, and the Reign of Law (our systems of Universal Gravitation and Cosmic Evolution) were tersely summed up in the famous axiom of the Smagdarine Tablet of Hermes: 'That which is below is as that which is above, and that which is above is as that which is below.' This basic concept they expressed in various ways, as by ascribing to their rulers celestial descent while associating their great deeds with appropriate constellations, and, in Egypt if not elsewhere, by laying out the land, dividing its districts, and naming its cities in allusion to astronomy, a course which Drummond makes it appear probable, from an etymological examination of Hebrew names of places and persons, the twelve tribes of Israel pursued when they entered the promised land, bearing the twelve signs of the Zodiac for tribal emblems.

20. "From this point of view it appeared remarkable, so far as the present writer could ascertain, no pyramid student had surmised that possibly in the Great Pyramid we possess the connecting link between the astronomy and the geography of the ancients. Such a connecting link, if recovered, would naturally be expected to determine, incidentally, the long-lost equal-measurement boundaries of the zodiacal constellations; and if it should further prove to be the link between the science and the religion of the ancients, then possibly something might be discovered in the line of

Schelling's brilliant hypothetical surmise: 'How if, in mythologoy, the ruins of a superior intelligence, and even a perfect system, were found, which would reach far beyond the horizon which the most ancient written records present to us." *

21. This is just what we have found. In the Supreme Initiation of the Mystic and Occult Masonry we *have* this Key. Not only have we the Key, but we have found the "Lost Word" which the Master Mason Degree teaches us was lost. There is no longer any guess work in this, but it is a *fact* as any Master Mason may prove for himself. In its Degrees are the *absolute* secrets of all Religions and every Initiate becomes a Priest. This is possibly a bold claim to make in the present age of materialism, but to me it is a question whether even the Ministers of the Gospel have formed any idea that the present age of Materialism is to give way, *within the near future,* to a Science-Religion or Religion-Science?

22. "The round churches of the Templars were built in circular or cyclar (i.e. Gilgal) form in allusion to astronomical facts. All the round chapter-houses and choirs were built round for the same reason the churches of the Templars were built round. In the chapter-houses and crypts, till the thirteenth century, the secret religion, perpetuating the relics of a science *not* falsely so-called, was celebrated in safe seclusion from the profane and ignorant vulgar. The *eternal* ethical truths deduced by the grandest minds, from the astronomical events connected with the history of the

* Parsons, "New Light from the Great Pyramid."

planetary fractricide were communicated to the common people in the nave (navy) of the church, as the ark of salvation, in allegories like that of Hagar (Gal. IV). Thus the Initiates sought to bring within the reach of the *humblest* minds, the *fruits* of the most difficult sciences and the most ancient learning.

23. "The secret (i.e., "Sacred"), religion arose from the natural and insuperable difficulty of communicating the great truths of astronomy to the ignorant, and of preserving records of the great phenomena of nature. Without universal relations no ethic, but only expediency, is possible. All the mystery and allegory grew upon the necessity of using symbols and characters by which the skilled might communicate with each other, but which the ignorant ran away with. And as they were infinitely in the majority, the learned found their symbols taken out of their own hands, and they were not allowed to rectify the errors of general ignorance, nor to explain their *own* meaning." *

24. The Secret Orders *never* had any intention of being as secret as they are. Priests of the Religion were only too willing to teach the people, but the people *were no more willing to receive the truth then than they are now.* The *accusation by religious* systems that the secret Orders are of the devil because they do not admit all, Initiated and uninitiated, is utterly false. It is not the Men of these Orders that exclude the people from them. *It is the people themselves*

---

* Parsons, "New Light from the Great Pyramid."

through their ignorance, that excludes them. The Priests of the *genuine* Orders have learned long ago as the Christ taught: "Cast not pearl before swine, lest they trample upon them." All Orders are open to the people if they are willing to learn. Mystic Masonry opens its door to Supreme Initiation, but it cannot take the ignorant on the same footing as the learned, for he who knows not the A. B. C. of Education cannot become the teacher of Latin, nor can the ignorant of Religion and Philosophy become the teacher of these systems. The Secret Orders are open to those *who are willing to learn and obey until such time as they are able to take care of themselves.*

25. All Masonry deals largely with ethics and symbolism of the Ancient Mysteries. The writer believes that through the well-timed efforts of Masons to-day the grandest achievements in knowledge ever gained by man, which were originally concealed in the Greater Mysteries of Antiquity, and in time became lost to the world, may again be recovered. *In the strictest sense this knowledge has never really been lost, as there have always existed those who were possessed of the great secret.* It was originally veiled in order to conceal it from the profane, and written in a universal language of Symbolism that the wise among *all* nations and throughout *all* time might read it, as it were, in their own language. It was also written in parable and allegory, so that the unlettered and common people might not be deprived of its wise precepts, and of its force in shaping character, dissipating ignorance, and inspiring hope. This Ancient Wisdom is the founda-

tion from which *(all)* Masonry takes its rise. The *true* Science of Symbolism in time became lost; the Temples of Initiation fell into decay, or were destroyed by priests and potentates, jealous of their influence. For many weary centuries men have been trying to recover the lost key and to restore the ancient wisdom from the parables and allegories in which it had been concealed.* But progress in this inverse order is not only necessarily slow and uncertain, but all such attempts have, more or less, given rise to fantastic flights of the imagination, and resulted in confusion, rather than in enlightenment. The result has been to bring the whole subject under contempt, and to make the name "mysticism" mean something vague and uncertain, if not altogether foolish, to those ignorant of its true meaning.

26. "It will be very naturally questioned whether any Greater Mysteries of Antiquity existed inasmuch as they were always concealed, never revealed to the profane, never published to the world, and only recorded in glyphic, parable and allegory. It has already been shown that all attempts to discover the real secret by running backward from parable and allegory have resulted in confusion and discouragement. The interpretations resulting have been as fantastic and varied as the genius of each investigator; had any of these been possessed of a universal key to symbolism, or a

*This "lost key" is fully and absolutely recovered in the degrees of Ancient and Mystic Oriental Masonry. Not only the Key to Wisdom Religion, but to Religion itself.

complete philosophy of the Secret Doctrine, the result might have been very different. The solution of this question is not only greatly simplified, when investigation is guided by such a philosophy, or a complete key, but the investigator has the positive assurance at every step that he is on firm ground." *

27. There has always been a tradition in the far East, and to be often traced more or less vaguely in the West, that the Great Lodge of the Magi, the Adepts, the Perfect Masters, known and designated also by many other names, has never ceased to exist; that this Lodge has often, though secret and unknown, shaped the course of Empires and controlled the fate of Nations.** That this is a fact beyond dispute has only lately been proven openly in the issueing of a Secret Mandate that the Secret Degrees of Mystic Oriental Masonry should be worked and by the appointment of a Deputy Grand Master in America by the Supreme Order of the Universe.

28. "Such work has now become possible, because of a cycle of liberality and enlightenment, when the workers are not likely to be sacrificed to the Moloch of bigotry and superstition. Granting that such Masters exist *(and they do exist)*, and that they are possessed of profound knowledge, that they are ready to help the world, the world must be ready and willing to receive such help, if it is to be benefited by it, instead of destroying its agents. Guided, then, by a complete

* Dr. Buck, "Mystic Masonry."
**See both "The Philosophy of Fire" and "The Rosicrucians."

3a

philosophy; armed with a key to symbolism, and aided by these Grand Masters, the Lost Mysteries of Antiquity may be restored and made to tell their hoary secrets for the benefit of the coming ages.

29. "Only the Perfect Master can so chip away the stone as to reveal in all its grandeur and beauty the *Divine Ideal*, and endow it with the breath of life. Such is the building of character. The fable of Pygmalion and Galatea, is, after all, more real than history. The thread of history is not in isolate facts, joined by conjecture, and warped to the ignorant, bigoted, and time-serving opinions of men. The real thread is to be sought in the *theme* that runs through the symphony of creation; in the lofty *ideals* that inspire the life of man, and that lead him from the clod and the lowlands, where hover the ghosts of superstition and fear to the mountains of light, where dwell forever inspiration and peace. Such ideals are the *Christ, Hiram,* and the *Perfect Masters.*

30. "No genuine Mason, imbued with the spirit of liberality, will treat any religion with derision or contempt, or exclude from fellowship any Brother who believes in the existence of God, the Brotherhood of Man and the Immortality of the Soul. This Catholic spirit is the very foundation of Masonry, and any departure from it is *un*-Masonic, and subversive of the ancient Landmarks and Genius of Masonry. True Masonry has, for ages, held aloft the torch-light of Toleration, Equity and Fraternity. The bigoted sectarian, whoever he may be, divides the world into two classes; those who, with zeal and blind faith, accept his dogmas

and those who do not.

31. "In its ritualism and monitorial lessons Masonry teaches nothing in morals, in science, in religion, or in any other department of human knowledge or human interest, not taught elsewhere in current forms of thought, or by the sages of the past. In these directions it has no secrets of any kind. It is in the ancient symbols of Freemasonry that its real secrets lie concealed, and these are as densely veiled to the Mason as to any other, unless he has studied the science of symbolism in general, and Masonic symbols in particular. In place of the term Mystic Masonry, the term Symbolic Masonry might have been used alone, but just here lies the whole secret, a profound mystery, and few Masons up to the present time have had the interest or the patience necessary to such investigation. This is a fact, and not intended as either a criticism or a reproach. If lacking a knowledge of the profound meaning of Masonic symbolism, and its transcendent interest and importance, Masons have allowed the whole organization not only to fail in all real progress, but to degenerate, that is indeed a reproach.

32. "There was never greater need than at the present time; never so great an opportunity as now for Masonry to assume its true place among the institutions of man and to force recognition by the simple power of Brotherly Love, Relief, and Truth, based upon philosophy such as nowhere else exists outside of its ancient symbols. If the majority of Masons do not realize the true significance and value of their possessions, there is all the more need for those who do to

speak out, even in the face of discouragement and detraction, and do their utmost to demonstrate the truth. Does any intelligent Mason imagine that the guilds of practical Masons of a century and a half ago originated the order of Freemasons? There were indeed Architects, and Master builders among them, but the great majority of Masons were far more ignorant, as manual servants, than the majority of such builders are to-day.

33. "Freemasonry is modeled on the plan of Ancient Mysteries, with their glyphics and allegories, and this is no mere coincidence; the parallels are too closely drawn. Bro. Pike came to the conclusion, after long and patient investigation, that certain Hermetic Philosophers* had a hand in the construction of the organization of Free and Accepted Masons, and if they embodied in its symbolism more than appears on the surface, and far deeper truths than the superficial student really discerns, it was evidently designed that future generations should discern and use these profounder secrets.

34. "In brief, then, the *real* Secrets of Freemasonry lie in its Symbols, and the meaning of the symbols reveal a profound philosophy, and a Universal Science, that have never been transcended by man."

35. "There is a thread of tradition connecting modern Masonry with the most ancient Mysteries of Antiquity. The ancient landmarks may be discovered in every

---

*For further information, see "The Rosicrucians; their Teachings."

nation and time. 'Notwithstanding the connection
that so evidently exists,' says Dr. Rebold, 'between the
Ancient Mysteries and the Freemasonry of our day,
the latter should be considered an initiation rather
than a continuation of those ancient Mysteries; for
initiation into them was the entering of a school,
wherein were taught art, science, morals, law, philosophy, philanthropy and the wonders and worship of
(the Symbols) nature.' "*

36. The universal Science and Sublime Philosophy,
once taught in the Greater Mysteries of Atlantis,
Egypt, Chaldea, Persia and India, has been a dead
letter in modern Freemasonry, but these Sciences and
this Sublime Philosophy is taught in Mystic Masonry
as it never was in the Ancient Mysteries. The candidate can become proficient in the Ancient Wisdom if
he is willing to do so. Nothing of the Ancient
Mysteries will be withheld from those who are willing
to learn.

37. "It should be borne in mind that in modern
Freemasonry, in the Ancient Mysteries, and in *all* the
great Religions, there was always an Exoteric portion
given out to the world, to the uninitiated, and an
Esoteric portion reserved for the Initiate, and revealed (only) in the *degrees*, according as the candidate demonstrated his fitness to receive, conceal, and
rightly use the knowledge so imparted. Few professed
Christians are, perhaps, aware that such was the case

---

* Dr. Buck, "Mystic Masonry."

with Christianity during the first two or three centuries."*

38. "This, in its *purity*, as taught by Christ himself,
was the true primitive religion, as communicated by
God to the Patriarchs. It was no new religion, but the
reproduction of the oldest of all; and its true and perfect morality is the morality of (true) Masonry, as it
is the morality of *every* creed of antiquity."**

39. Says St. Augustine: "What is now Called the
Christian Religion existed among the ancients, and
was not absent from the human race until Christ
came, from which time the true religion, which existed
already, began to be called Christian."***

40. "In the early days of Christianity, there *was* an
initiation like those of the Pagans. Persons were
admitted on special conditions only. To arrive at a
complete knowledge of the doctrine, they had to pass
three degrees of instructions."****

41. There was an exoteric and an esoteric doctrine
with the early Christians; the esoteric doctrines were
communicated orally in the Mysteries of Initiation;
and these Mysteries conformed to and were originally
derived from those of the so-called Pagan world. The
Mysteries of Christ received a new interpretation
after the first Nicene Council, and as the Church
sought dominion, it lost the Great Secret, and since

---

* Dr. Buck, "Mystic Masonry."
** Albert Pike, "Morals and Dogma."
*** Heckthorne, "Secret Societies."
**** Albert Pike, "Morals and Dogma."

then has and does, deny that it ever existed, and has
done, and is doing, all in its power to obliterate all its
records and monuments.

42. Neither Christianity of to-day nor modern Freemasonry is the direct and lineal descendant of the
Greater Mysteries of Antiquity or Supreme Initiation,
the Fraternity of the Rosy Cross and Ancient Mystic
Masonry *alone* have preserved the Key of interpretation. Modern Masonry never possessed this key but
may if they are willing to accept the terms.

43. "Modern Freemasonry honors as its ancient
great teachers Zoroaster, Pythagoras, Plato, and many
others, and in some of its degrees gives a brief summary of their doctrines. Masonry, in a certain sense,
includes them all, and has adopted their precepts.
They were all initiates in the Mysteries, and funda-
mentally, their doctrines were the same. All taught
the existence of the G. A. O. U., the Immortality of the
Soul, and the unqualified Brotherhood of Man; and
with these primitive and fundamental truths Masonry
is in ful laccord."*

44. "The Entered Apprentice starts on his career
with the triangle surmounting the square (spirit has
not yet descended into matter). As he progresses the
descent takes place, and we have the triangle in the
square, and finally as a Master the ascent of the square
into the triangle begins, which every Master Mason
will understand. Masonry being a 'Progressive
Science,' the progress of the neophyte is thus made to

---

* Dr. Buck, "Mystic Masonry."

conform to the process of evolution and the descent
of spirit into matter, and this is illustrated by the
manner in which he is taught to wear his apron in
each degree in the Blue Lodge. The Entered Apprentice is *not* only a 'hewer of wood and a drawer of
water,' but is a novice, taking his first instruction, and
this is symbolized by his apron.

45. "The tradition of the Master's Word, of the
power which its possession gives to the Master; the
story of its loss and the search for its recovery; the
tradition of the Ineffable name in connection with the
Lost Word, showing that it could not or should not be
pronounced, except with bated breath; or, as the
Hindoo tradition declares, 'with the hand covering the
mouth.' The symbol of the three greater and three
lesser lights, and the play made in many places on the
word *Light* itself, in conjunction with the Lost Word,
all these references and uses constitute a complicated
Symbolism working in and towards a common center
or glyphic, which, taken in conjunction with the building and restoration of the Temple constitute the secret
Symbolism of Masonry, and illustrate the whole
process of Initiation. What real Initiation is, has
already been stated. These symbols when correctly
interpreted, serve two purposes. First, they reveal a
complete philosophy of the Creation of the Universe
and of Man, unfolding all essences, powers, and
potencies, and their mutual relations and correlations.
Second, they unfold the process of Initiation as synonymous with the uninterrupted evolution of man
guided by knowledge and design along the lines of

least resistance. In the third degree the candidate impersonates *Hiram*, who has been shown to be identical with the *Christos* of the Greeks, and with the Sun-Gods of all other nations. The superiority of Masonry at this point over all other exoteric Religions consists in this: All these religions take the *symbol for the thing symbolized*. Christ was originally *like* the Father. Now He is made *identical* with the Father... Here lies the true meaning of *Abiff*, 'of, or from my Father.' Hiram—*Chistos*, and Abiff—'at one with the Father,' i. e., 'of,' or 'from.' In deifying Jesus the whole of humanity is bereft of *Christos* as an eternal potency *within* every human soul, a latent Christ in every man. In thus deifying one man, they have orphaned the whole of humanity. On the other hand, Masonry, in making every candidate personify *Hiram*, has preserved the original teaching, which is a Universal Glyphic. Few candidates may be aware that Hiram, whom they have represented and personify, is ideally, and precisely the same as Christ. Yet such is the case. This old philosophy shows what Christ as a glyphic means, and how the Christ-state results from real Initiation, or from the evolution of the human *into* the Divine. Regeneration is thus given a meaning that is both apprehensible and attainable; both philosophical and scientific; *and at once ideal and practical*. In the Tetragrammation, or four-lettered name of Deity, the Greek followers of Pythagoras found a glyphic by which they both expressed and concealed their philosophy, and it is the Hebrew tetrad IHVH, or 'Yod, he, vau, he,' that is introduced into Masonry with the Pythagorean art speech. The devout Hebrew, in reading the sacred text, when he came to the tetral IHVH, substituted the word *Adonai* (Lord), and if the word was written the points of Alhim, he called it Elohim. This custom is preserved in Masonry by giving the candidate a substitute for the Master's Word. The Hebrew tetrad 'Yod, he, vau, he,' is produced by repeating the 'he.' The root word is a triad, and the quaternary is undoubtedly a blind. The Sacred word is found in the Mysteries as a binary, a trinary, and a quaternary; as with the Hindoos we have the *om*, and the *a, u, m,* indicating different methods of pronouncing the Sacred name.'*

46. This Secret of the Lost Word is carried on and fully explained in the Higher Degrees of Mystic Masonry and as already stated, the Candidate is taught not only the meaning of The Sacred Name or Lost Word, but *is taught the Word itself*.

47. "The Secret Doctrine is the Complete Philosophy of Masonic Symbolism. So long as this philosophy is unknown to the Mason, his symbols are, to a great extent, dead letters. The work of the lodge a dumb show beyond its moral precepts, and the Genius of Masonry for the members of the Craft is largely the spirit of self-interest, mutual support, and physical enjoyment or revelry, the latest embodiment of which is the 'Mystic Shrine.' But there are some among the members of the Craft—and how many time alone can determine—who believe that Masonry means far more

---

*Dr. Buck, ''Mystic Masonry.

than this, and who have already discerned in its
symbols and traditions something of their real meaning. Many of these have found partial clues which
served to keep interest alive while searching for
plainer meanings and deeper revelations. In retracing
the steps which these ancient symbols and their profound philosophy have come down to our own times,
more and more obscured with every passing century,
students have gathered a large number of facts, a great
mass of traditions and general information, all of
which have been variously interpreted by different
writers on Masonry. All writers, however, agree in
the conclusions that the symbols and traditions of
Freemasonry come from the far East, and go back to
the remotest antiquity." *

48. "After the candidate is obligated and brought
to Light in the third degree, he is bantered with the
statement that undoubtedly he now imagines himself
a Master Mason. He is informed not only that such is
not the case, but that there is no certainty that he ever
will become such. He subsequently starts on his journey
for the discovery of the Lost Word. The method by
which he undertakes to obtain it, and the names of the
three Fellow-crafts, have a very deep significance. After many trials, he receives a substitute, which he is to
conceal with great fidelity "till future generations
shall discover the Lost Word."**

49. "The method by which he receives and is ever

* Dr. Buck, "Mystic Masonry."

**In the Rites of Mystic Masonry the Lost Word is
not only found but taught the Candidate.

to transmit or use even the substitute, is made exact
and definite; and guarded by solemn obligations. The
meaning of both the great secrecy and the use of the
word are left entirely to conjecture, beyond the statement that it is a sacred name, and must never be
profaned or taken in vain, or carelessly used; and I
venture the opinion. that *not one Mason among ten
thousand has ever been able to discover why.*

50. "The force of the obligation is therefore in the
obligation and not in the reason. As a matter of fact, the
real reason is scientific to the last analysis; scientific
to a degree beyond the penetration, up to the present
time, of the 'radiant matter' of the *Roentgen Ray* of
Modern Science. The *Word* concerns the science of
rhythmic vibrations, and is the key to the equilibrium
of all forces and to the harmony of Eternal Nature.

51. "This tradition of the *Ineffable Name* is brought
into Masonry from the Hebrew Kabalah, and how it
became lost is part historical, at least. The ancient
Hebrew Priests evidently undertook to fit to the names
of their tribal-deities the symbolism and traditions of
the far East. If the Master's Word was really a *word*
at all, the Deity of the Hebrews might perhaps represent it as well as any other. It is a question of pro-
netics, however, rather than mere orthography. Beneath the Hebrew text of the Pentateuch lies concealed
the science of the Kabalah. The Anathemas threatened
for him who should alter, by a single letter or 'Yod,'
the outer text, had therefore a deeper meaning. The
priests of many nations of antiquity were initiates in
the Mysteries, and as such they were Monotheists,

while the ignorant masses were idolaters. The monotheism of the Jews was of a robust character, and their priests and prophets had a hard time to preserve their people from the seductive polytheism and abominations of surrounding nations. The Ineffable Name was not only concealed, but 'terrible as an army with banners.' Jehovah was jealous, revengeful, vindictive towards the evil-doer, tolerated no rival in the broad expanse of Cosmos. In no religion of antiquity is the anthropomorphic image of Deity so strongly defined, and the Creator of man and worlds made so exceedingly human.

52. "The Kabalah, on the contrary, embodying considerable of the true and ancient Secret Doctrine, held a different idea of Divinity. While carrying the tradition, therefore, of the lost word as the Ineffable Name of Deity, the symbolism was taken as literal fact, and the people who were commanded to 'make no graven image' ended by making a gigantic idol, half Moloch and half Man. Amid such contradictions, the symbolism adopted from the purer and gentler Aryans was ill at ease and far from home. Rev. Dr. Garrison claims in a 'Contribution to the History of the Lost Word,' appended to Foot's *Early History and Antiquities of Freemasonry,* that the four-syllabled name, Jehovah, was held by the Hebrews as the *Ineffable,* and that Adonai was used as a substitute. The High Priests once every year, at the time of the atonement, entered alone into the Holy of Holies and there repeated the name. The name was thus withdrawn from and finally lost by the common people. This is in-

genious and too literal to cover the case. The old query, 'What is in a name?' is, after all, not so easy of answer; or the answer might be, 'everything or nothing,' according as you understand it or look at it. Before the introduction of the Masoretic points or indices of vowel sounds, the consonants were read by metrically intoning the text. The principle of the Mantram was therefore known to the High Priests at least, and, therefore, the Word, the Name, that known in all its pentitude and used with power, '*caused the whole world to shake*,' may have been used or invoked in the Holy of Holies by the Kabalistic Hierophant. Some who read this may be even yet so ignorant of the potency of sound as to smile at the credulity and gullibility that indites it; and yet so superstitious over the *letters of a name* as to believe them more sacred in one form than another. Notwithstanding, it is the letter that killeth, and the Spirit (the breath) that maketh alive. The consonants composing the Hebrew alphabet are about as sacred as so many wooden blocks. If one knows how to arrange the blocks, and endow them with life, so that they may 'bud and blossom like Aaron's rod,' that of course is a very different matter.

53. "The traditional Lost Word of the Master is a Key to all the science of Magic. The knowledge of the Master is *not* empirical. It does not consist of a few isolated formula by which certain startling or unusual effects can be produced. The Magician's art is based on a science far more deep and exact than modern physical science has yet dreamed of, and back

of this science lies a philosophy as boundless as Cosmos, as inexhaustible as Time, and as beneficient as the 'Father in Heaven.' If the Masonic meaning of *Master, Perfect and Sublime Master, Prince Adept,* etc., is less than I have indicated, then it is a roaring farce, or a stupendous humbug. The conception of Masonry is true, but it has adopted or imitated the ritual and glyphics of a science, the Key to which not one Mason in ten thousand possesses, and hence the tradition of the Lost Word has a literal, no less than a symbolical meaning. The 'Substitute' is given to the neophyte—'till future generations shall find the True Word.' The question now propounded to every 'obligated,' or so-called Master Mason, is—is the present, the generation in which that which was lost shall be found? and each must answer for himself singly; just as he entered the Lodge, first saw the light, and took his obligation; just as every *real* Master, or 'White Adept,' has done since the beginning of time. There exists in Masonic literature many learned essays on the history, orthography and philology of the *Lost Word;* but I am acquainted with no treatise that apprehends the nature of the *real* secret like that of Brother Albert Pike in his great work, and yet, if he knew the whole secret, he concealed it at last.

54. "The True Word of a Mason is to be found in the concealed and profound meaning of the *Ineffable Name* of *Deity* communicated by God to Moses" (rather to the Priests of Ancient Atlantis), "and which meaning was long lost by the very precautions taken to conceal it. The true pronunciation of that

name was in truth a secret, in which, however, was involved the far more profound secret of its meaning.''

55. ''Thus the Ineffable Name not only embodies the great Philosophical Idea, that the Deity is the *Ens,* the *To on* the absolute Existence, that of which the Essence is To Exist, the only Substance of Spinoza, the *Being,* that never could not have existed, as contra-distinguished from that which only becomes; not Nature or the Soul of Nature, but that which created Nature; but also the idea of the Male and Female Principles, in its highest and most profound sense: to wit, that God originally comprehended in Himself all that is; that matter was not co-existent with Him or independent of Him; that He did not merely fashion and shape a pre-existing chaos into a universe; but that *His Thought* manifested itself outwardly in that universe, which so became, and before was not, except as comprehended in Him; that the Generative Power, or Spirit, and the Productive Matter, ever among the ancients deemed the Female, originally were in God, and that He Was and Is all that Was, that Is, and that Shall be; in whom all else lives, moves, and has its being.''

56. ''This was the great Mystery of the Ineffable Name, and of course its *true* pronunciation and its meaning became lost to all except the select few to whom it was confided; it being concealed from the common people, because the Deity, thus metaphysically named, was not that personal and capricious, and as it were, tangible God in whom they believed, and who alone was within reach of their crude capacities.

......This was the profound truth hidden in the ancient allegory and covered from the general view with a double veil. This was the exoteric meaning of the generation and production of the Indian, Chaldéan, and Phoenician Cosmogonies; of the Active and Passive Powers; of the Male and Female Principles; of Heaven and its Luminaries generating, and the Earth producing; all hidden from vulgar view, as above its comprehension; the doctrine that matter is not eternal, but that God was the only Original Existence, the Absolute, from Whom everything has proceeded, and to Whom all returns. And this True Word is with entire accuracy said to have been lost, because its meaning was lost even among the Hebrews, although we still find the name (its real meaning unsuspected) in the Hu of the Druids and Fo-Hi of the Chinese.''

57. "The Holy Bible is one of the *great* Lights in Masonry and has a very profound meaning when coupled with the tradition of the Ineffable Name, or Lost Word. The object set before the neophyte in his search for the Lost Word, is, that he may travel in foreign countries and receive Master's wages, which are Knowledge and Power. The glyphic in its outer form is taken from the guilds of practical Masons of two or three centuries ago. The laws then governing the Mark of a Fellowcraft or a Master Builder were very strict, and the Mark was never bestowed unworthily, and when received was a passport among builders over a wide domain. But in a deeper, or Kabalistic sense, the Master's Word, which entitled

its possessor to Master's wages, was a very different
thing indeed. The wages of the *real* Master were the
satisfaction and the power that flow from the possession of real knowledge. Knowledge is power only
when one comprehends that which he possesses, and
is, therefore, enabled to use it for the purposes that
lie nearest his heart. Albert Pike shows conclusively
that the power of the *word* lies in the knowledge of
the Philosophy which is its perfect synthesis. This is,
in part, the meaning of 'knowing how to pronounce
the Word.'

58. "As already stated, the Kabalah of the Ancient
Hebrews, which Moses derived by initiation into the
Mysteries of Egypt and Persia, and which Albert Pike
and many others declare was identical among the Hebrews, the Egyptians, Hindoos and other nations of
antiquity, was known as the *secret doctrine*. The reason for such a name is fully revealed in what has been
shown hitherto.

59. "What Albert Pike says regarding the relation
of the Pentateuch to the Kabalah, is true of the exoteric scriptures of every nation of antiquity."*

60. Mystic Masonry has come to teach the *inner*
truths of Masonry, and there is no doubt but that it
will fulfill its mission completely and ere many years
have passed away.

61. "The traditions, glyphics and ritual of Freemasonry cluster around the building of the temple;
the legend of the Widow's son, Hiram-abiff, who lost

---

* Dr. Buck, "Mystic Masonry."

his life in the defense of his integrity, and the search
for the Lost Word of the Master. As the candidate
progresses, degree after degree, he is furnished with
the working tools suited to his degree of knowledge
and proficiency, given instructions as to their use;
the lesser and greater *lights* are revealed and explained; and through all, each outer form, or material
thing, is shown to be a symbol of a deeper mystery, a
concealed potency.

62. "This is, in brief, the language and the philosophy of symbolism, or the exoteric, and the esoteric
garb of Truth. The method itself, outside of all details or applications, has a deeper scientific significance than most persons are aware of. This method
of instruction is *not* fanciful or arbitrary, but con-
forms to the process of the Eternal Nature in building an atom or a world; a daisy or a man. Cosmos
has evolved from Chaos, and yet Chaos remains the
Eternal Potency; what Plato called the *'world of divine ideas.'* This will be more fully explained in another part........The essential form, or *idea* of all
things; the potency or force; and the matter as we
now discern it, must have existed in primordial space.
Therefore, these two always exist, viz., the inner potency, and the outer act; the concealed Idea, and the
outer form; the inner meaning, and the outer event.
Each in its turn a symbol of the other. Hence the
saying on the Smaragdine Tablet, *as above so below.*
All outward things are, therefore, symbols, or embodi-
ments of pre-existing Ideas, and out of this subjective
ideal realm all visible things have *emanated.*

63. "This doctrine of emanations is the key to the philosophy of Plato, and that of the Gnostic sects from which the early Christians derived their *mysteries*. This fact is mentioned here in order to show the deep foundations of the glyphics of Masonry."[*]

64. "In the Ritual of Masonry, King Solomon's temple is *taken as a symbol*. The building and the restoration of the temple at Jerusalem are dramatically represented in the work of the Lodge, and in the ceremony of initiation, by a play upon words and parity of events, and applied to the candidate, with admonition, warning or encouragement, as the drama unfolds.

65. "The symbolism is fitted to Ideal relations, rather than to actual existences or historical events. Sol-om-on represents the name of Deity in three languages, and the Biblical history is an allegory or myth of the Sun-god. There is no reliable history of the construction of any such temple at Jerusalem, and recent explorations and measurements have greatly altered the dimensions as heretofore given.

66. "The *real* temple referred to from first to last in Masonry, as in all ancient initiations, is the Tabernacle of the Human Soul.

67. "It is built, indeed, without the sound of hammer or any tool of iron. It is like (made in the likeness of,) that other, *spiritual temple*, not made with hands, eternal in the heaven; for the old philosophy (Kabalah) teaches that the Immortal Spirit of man is

---

[*]Dr. Buck, "Mystic Masonry."

the Artificer of the body and its source of life; that it does not so much enter in, as overshadow man, while the Soul, the immediate vehicle of the Spirit, inhabits the body, and is dissipated at death. The Spirit is Immortal, pure, and forever underfiled. It is *Christos*, or *Hiram*, the Mediator between the Soul, or physical man, and the Universal Spirit—the Father in Heaven. The 'poor, blind Candidate,' that is, the man of sense, immersed in matter, would learn the *Ineffable Name*, and obtain the Lost Word, and, seeking a short-cut, 'climbs up some other way.' He would have wisdom without self-conquest, power without sacrifice. He will not listen to the voice of pleading. 'Be patient, my brother, and when the temple is completed, if found worthy, you shall receive that for which you have so long wrought.' No! he will have it *now!* and he silences the pleading voice, and, defeating only himself, flees into the deserts of remorse and calls upon the rocks to hide him from the pursuit of his accusing conscience. Hiram (*Christos*) is resurrected. Being immortal, he can not really die. No sin of man is final. Realizing his error and purified by suffering, the spirit of man being again lifted up, even defeat gives promise of victory, and he receives a Substitute for the Lost Word. He hears, however, faint or dim, the Divine Harmony. Future generations, that is, further trials and more sincere endeavor, promise greater reward. He learns to 'know, to will, to dare, and to keep silent.' Brotherly Love, Relief and Truth, Prudence, Fortitude, Justice and Mercy—all the virtues and all the Beatitudes are inculcated.

68. "The candidate is taught, not merely to tolerate another's religion, but to respect it as his own; though still adhering to that into which he was born. To make reasonable this obligation, he is shown through the Kabalah or Secret Doctrine that, at the heart of every great religion, lie the same eternal truths. Forms and observances only differ. The *Ineffable Name* is spelled in many ways, yet the Word is one and eternal. Masonry is not only a universal science, but a world-wide religion, and owes allegiance to no one creed, and can adopt no sectarian dogma, as such, without ceasing thereby to be Masonic. Drawn from the Kabalah, and taking the Jewish or Christian verbiage or symbols, it but discerns in them universal truths, which it recognizes in all other religions. Many degrees have been Christianized only to perish; as every degree eventually will if circumscribed by narrow creeds, and dwarfed to the apprehension, so as to exclude good men of any other communion. Is Jesus any the less *Christos,* because Christna was called 'the Good Shepherd?' or because the Mexican Christ was crucified between two thieves? Or, because Hiram was three days in a grave before he was resurrected? Are we not as selfish in our religion as in our other possessions? Then why is man, while cherishing as his most sacred possession, the religion of his fathers, eternally seeking to degrade and destroy that of his Brother?

69. "The Great Republic, to which Bro. Pike refers, is the Ideal of Masonry; the Genius that hovers like a protecting angel over the Lodge. Make it impossible·

for a Jew or Parsee, Buddhist or Brahmin, to enter
any Lodge without witnessing the profanation of his
sacred altars or contempt for his religion, and the
angel hides her face and retreats from altars already
profaned by unbrotherliness. Masonry is the Universal Religion only because, and only so long, as it embraces all religions. For this reason, and this alone, it
is universal and eternal. Neither persecution nor mis-
representation can ever destroy it. It may find no
place in a generation of bigots; it may retire for a
century; but again comes a Master Builder with the
Key to the 'Shut Palace of the King,' throws open the
blinds, lets in the light, kindles anew the fire on the
sacred altar, clears away the rubbish, when behold!
the tesselated pavement is as bright as when it first
came from the quarries of truth, the jewels are of
pure gold and brighten at the touch, and the great
lights are undimmed and undecayed. 'When the candidate is ready, the Master appears.' And yet men
are so foolish and so vile as to imagine that they can
destroy their heirloom of the ages; this heritage from
the Immortals! No age is so dark as to quench entirely the light of the Lodge; no persecution so bloody
as to blot out its votaries; no anathemas of Popes so
lasting as to count one second on its Dial of Time!
These, one and all, serve only to keep the people in
darkness, and retard the reign of Universal Brotherhood. Therefore for humanity—the Great Orphan--
the real Master laments. He smiles at the passions of
Popes or Kings and pities the folly of man. He *only
waits*, indifferent as to results, knowing these to be

under eternal law, but ready and willing, whenever and wherever the instruction entering the listening ear may find lodgment in the faithful breast. For ages, Kings, Popes and Synods have done their best to kill this Secret Doctrine by anathematizing or burning its Masters. The Jesuits got possession of its Lodges, transformed out of all recognition many of its degrees, and made of them an abject tool of the Sacerdotal hierarchy."

70. "Hiram Abiff is dramatically represented to have lost his life when the temple was near completion, and yet it is recorded that after the completion of the temple he labored for years to construct and ornament a palace for the King. Add to these facts the statement that the temple was constructed without the sound of hammer or any tool or iron, and it is thus likened more nearly to that other '*spiritual temple*, not made with hands, eternal in the heavens,' and the literal and historical features disappear, and the symbolism stands out in bold relief." *

71. "Masonic Lodges are dedicated to the Sts. John; one of whom, the Evangelist, opens his Gnostic Gospel with the Greek philosophy of the Logos, the principle of emanation already referred to; and the other, the Seer of Patmos, writes a book symbolical of ancient initiations, which many a non-initiate has tried in vain to interpret. It may thus be seen that there is a deep significance in the dedication of Lodges to

---

* Dr. Buck, "Mystic Masonry."

the Sts. John. Take, for example, Revelations xvi, 16:
'And the city lieth four-square, and the length is as
large as the breadth; and he measured the city with
the reed, twelve thousand furlongs. The length, and
the breadth and the height of it are equal.' (A perfect cube.) 'And he measured the wall thereof, a
hundred and forty and four cubits, according to the
measure of a man, that is an angel.' The language is
evidently a veil, designed to conceal the *real* meaning
from the uninitiated. As the measure of man; that is,
a *perfect* man, or 'angel,' we have the cubic as a symbol of perfect proportion. Hence a *square man.* The
temple of Sol-om-on, the Cubical City—which unfolded becomes a *cross,*—and hence, the 'measure of a
man'—all these refer to the work of *regeneration,* or
initiation. The rebuilding of the temple after the
plan drawn upon the Tressel-board, by which it shall
be like that spiritual temple, *not made with hands,*
plainly refers to initiation from which result perfect
proportion and perfect harmony."*

72. "A very limited knowledge of the history of
primitive worship and Mysteries is necessary to enable any person to recognize in the Master Mason,
Hiram, the Osiris of the Egyptians, the Mithras of the
Persians, the Bacchus of the Greeks, the Atys of the
Phrygians, of which these people celebrated the passion, death and resurrection, as Christians celebrate
to-day that of Jesus Christ. Otherwise, this is the
eternal and unvarying type of all the religions which
have succeeded each other upon the earth.

* Dr. Buck, "Mystic Masonry."

73. "In an astronomical connection, Hiram is the representative of the Sun, the symbol of his apparent progress, which appearing at the south gate, so to speak, is smote downward and more downward as he advances toward the west, which passing, he is immediately vanquished and put to death by darkness, represented, in following the same allegory by the spirit of evil; but, returning, he rises again, conqueror and resurrected." *

74. "Khurum, therefore, improperly called Hiram, is Khur-om, the same as *Her-ra, Hermes,* and *Heracles,* the personification of Light and the Sun, the Mediator, Redeemer and Savior."

75. "It is merely absurd to add the word, '*Abif,*' or '*Abiff,*' as part of the name of the architect. *Abin* (which we read Abif) means 'of my father's.'...... 'formerly one of my father's servants' or 'slave.'" **

76. "Modern Masonry being but an imitation of Ancient *genuine* Mysteries, the writer has no design of reading into it a meaning which cannot be fully verified. For the greater part, modern Masons are dealing with symbols, the Key for the *real* interpretation of which they never possessed, or even suspected that it existed. It remains for the future to determine whether any considerable number of our Masonic Brethren really desire to possess in fuller measure the Living Truth which the dead-letter text conceals. That Living Truth exists, and is as accessible to every

---

* Reybold, "History of Freemasonry."
** Albert Pike, "Morals and Dogma."

Mason as is the dead-letter or the dumb-show under
which it masquerades in every Lodge." *

77. "The genuine *Acacia* also is the thorny tama-
risk, the same tree which grew up around the body of
Osiris. It is a sacred tree among the Arabs, who made
of it the Idol Al-Uzza, which Mohammed destroyed.
It is abundant as a bush in the desert of Thur, and of
it the 'crown of Thorns' was composed, which was
set on the forehead of Jesus of Nazareth. It is a fit
type of Immortality on account of its tenacity of life;
for it has been known, when planted as a door-post, to
take root and shoot out budding boughs above the
threshold." **

---

* Dr. Buck, "Mystic Masonry."
** Albert Pike, "Morals and Dogma."

THE FOUNDATION OF ALL MASONRY

AND THE

ANCIENT MYSTERIES ARE ONE

The Order of the Architects of Africa or the African Brothers

Founded As Such 1767.*

78. This Order was composed of educated and well-principled brothers. Their lodges, in Europe, were all closed, except that of Constantinople, and even that was closed in the past century.

79. Only one of the Grand Masters was known; this was the councillor of war, Koeppen, who was also a Rosicrucian.

78. Their first degree offered a more extensive and complete instruction than all the degrees of the Scotch systems together. They said, and rightly so, that the Lodges of St. John neglected the great end, and that instruction was hardly to be had there, and that the Strict Observance did not know the grounds of the continuation of the Masonic Order. They occupied themselves with hieroglyphics, especially with those

---

*"*African Master Builders*. A secret society with a Masonic form which came into being about the year

relating to Freemasonry, which they sought to know well. They made a mystery of their goal up to the seventh degree, which could only be gained by zeal, perseverance and discretion. Their secondary occupations were the sciences, especially history and antiquities, the study of which they considered indispensable for the true Freemason.

1756, and ceased to exist 1786.* It professed to be devoted to the discovery of truth, and the cultivation of virtue, and was a very worthy and respectable order. They set forth that: 'When the architects were by wars reduced to a very small number, they determined to travel together into Europe, and there to form, together, new establishments. Many of them came into England with Prince Edward, son of Henry III, and were shortly afterwards called into Scotland by Lord Stewart. Their installation in this kingdom falls about the Masonic year 2307.' They received the protection of the King of Sweden in 1125, of the King of England in 1190, and of Alexander III, of Scotland, in 1284, There were five initiations into their Apprentice's degree: 1. The Apprentice to the Egyptian Secret, *Menes Musae*; 2. The initiation into the Egyptian Secret; 3. The Cosmopolite; 4. The Christian Philosopher; 5. The Lover of Truth The higher degrees followed these, of which there was three. *They had Chapters whose officers were chosen for life.*"**

*Contrary to what these authorities say, this Order never ceased to exist. It *did* change its name, but the Order remains in existance up to the present time. Only the initiates can know the history and then only those of the Higher Degrees.

**Macoy and Oliver "History and Cyclopedia of Freemasonry."

79. Their first degree was symbolically called the Architect or Apprentice of Egyptian secrets.

80. They called themselves the Africans, because their studies began with the history of the Egyptians, in whose mysteries they found indications of Freemasonry, although they placed its origin much later, as to which the Crusades gave them no light.

81. Their customs were simple and noble. They never laid any stress on decorations, aprons, ribbons, jewels, etc., but they liked a certain luxury, and sententious inscriptions with a sublime but *hidden* meaning. In their assemblies they read treatises and communicated to each other the result of their researches.

82. Their banquets were simple, decorum prevailed, and instructive and scientific discourses were given at them.

83. Admissions were given without fees. Earnest brothers who fell into distress received much assistance.

84. This Order was established in Prussia, 1767, with the assent of Frederick II., called the Great.

85. Its degrees, to the number of eleven, were divided into two temples, viz. :—

First Temple.

   1. Apprentice.

   2. Companion.

   3. Master.

This First Temple, under Mystic Masonry, is now known as the Blue Lodge.

   1. Apprentice.

   2. Fellow Craft.

3. Master Mason.

Second Temple.

4. Architect, or Apprentice of the Egyptian Secrets.

(Manes Musae.)

5. Initiate in the Egyptian Secrets.

6. Cosmopolitan Brother.

7. Christian Philosopher (Bossinius).

8. Master of the Egyptian secrets, Alethophilote (Friend of Truth).

Higher degrees.

9. Armiger.

10. Miles.

11. Eques.

Under Mystic Masonry:—

4. Grand Master of the Secret Manuscript.

5. King's Pioneer.

6. Master of the Secret Cavern.

Higher Degrees.

The Four Degrees conferred in the King's Chamber in the Great Pyramid.

11. Name never mentioned or written before the profane world.

86. In the year 1806 only one Chapter of this system remained to the world and that at Berlin (Constantinople). From the continuation of the Chapter came the Grand Officers of the Ancient Mystic Oriental Masons as the Order is now known.

87. When Frederick II. came to the throne, seeing that Freemasonry was no longer what it had been, and appreciating what it might be, he conceived the plan of

an Inner Order or Circle, which might at the same
time take the place of a Masonic Academy. He made
choice of a certain number of Masons capable of comprehending his ideas, and charged them with the organization of this body. Among these were to be noticed the brothers Stahl, de Gone, Meyerotto and du
Bosc. *They instituted the Order under the name of an
extinct society,* The Architects of Africa, and established statutes in accordance with the views of the
King, who on his side granted privileges, and in 1768
had erected in Silesia, by his architect, Meil, a building
specially designed for the Grand Chapter, and endowed it with an ample fund, with a choice library
and rich furniture, the whole being of an elegance
worthy of the Order and of the Kind.

88. This Order, without pretending to dominion,
teaching tolerance, professing the primitive principles
of Freemasonry, and making a special study of its history, prospered in silence and in complete freedom.
Its chief statutes were to fear God only, to honor the
King and to be discreet, to exercise universal tolerance towards all Masonic sects without ever affiliating
itself to any. It was for this reason that they never
submitted to the act of obedience of the Baron de
Hund, notwithstanding all the entreaties that were
made to them to do so. In the admission of candidates they observed the strictest caution. It is said
that Duke Ferdinand of Brunswick was refused because he meddled with sectarian affairs. They devoted
themselves to active researches into the history of the
mysteries, the secret societies and their various
5a

branches, and cultivated the sciences, chiefly mathematics. In their works, carried on often in Latin, reigned morality, a high tone, a solid and unostentatious teaching.

89. Their library and their archives obtained through the protection of the King and of persons of distinction, among others the Prince von Lichtenstein, at Vienna, some real treasures of manuscripts and documents, which *no* Masonic branch can boast.

90. "Few monarchs have more thoroughly protected the Mystic Schools within the Masonic body than Frederick II., King of Prussia, well named 'The Great.' Not only did he protect them, but he also actively sympathized with them. While still Crown Prince, he was initiated as a Mason at Brunswick in August, 1738, and was from that period the staunch protector of the Masonic Fraternity; nor did he omit to penetrate very deeply into the early traditions of Masonry, far more so, indeed, than many who have fewer duties to engage their time.

91. "Frederick the Great, was, however, by no means, the vague and dreamy Mystic of popular representation; his Academy and Schools were the centers of the most brilliant intellects of the period, while the choice of his friends, literary, philosophical, and mystic, testifies to the breadth of his knowledge, and it also illustrates the manifold sympathies of his nature, both as a soldier and mystic, philosopher and scholar; though not saintly, by any means, he was thoroughly appreciative of ideals that were beyond him.

92. "His sympathy with mystics is evidenced by his

selection of a librarian, for he gave that post at the Royal Public Library in Berlin, with the title of Academician, to Don Anroine Joseph Pernetty, or Per-nty, a man who had been a Benedictine monk of the Congregation of Saint-Maur, but having become—like many others—dissatisfied with the Order, he applied to the Pope for a dispensation from his vows. This was no obstacle in the eyes of the King, deeply inter-ested as he was in the researches of this well-known Hermetist and Alchemist.''

93. That the opinions of Don Pernty were publicly known is demonstrated by a writer of the period, who says: *

94. ''A remarkable trait in the character of this Academician was, that he believed in the Philosopher's Stone, the mysteries of the Cabala, apparitions, pata-gonians, witches, enchantments, the race of giants, etc. But, notwithstanding this inconceivable and ri-diculous weakness, he was beloved by everyone, and the more as, to his other excellent qualities, he joined that of the most perfect discretion in regard to such affairs as were at any time confided to his secrecy; never did a word from his lips give room for the smallest explanation or disagreement.''

95. Such was the comment on this Mystic's charac-ter by one, who, while adverse to his opinions, never-theless, renders justice to a personality which some traduced.

96. Don Pernetty was for some time in personal re-

---

* Mrs. Cooper-Oaklet, ''Hidden Sources of Masonry.''

lationship with M. de St. Germain, the Rosicrucian; and later on, he founded the Academie des Illumines d'Avignon, in which the last Supreme Grand Master of the Ancient Mystic Oriental Masons was a student and which was essentially Hermetic in its aims, and had also a close connection with the Swedish system. This was a secret body, but it was also under the general Masonic regulations. It was also in close union with the followers of Martinez Pasquales, the founder of the *real* order of Martinists, and that bond has been kept up *because Martinez Pasquales was a member of the Mystic Masonic Body.*

97. "The most succinct account of the opinions held by the leading Freemasons in Germany at this juncture is given by Findel, who, although a pronounced antagonist, shows very lucidly the *underlying mystic* basis on which the outward Masonic forms were supported, and it is of value to these researches to quote his testimony in full, illustrating, as it unwittingly does, the hypothesis put forward, namely, that *all the Societies similar to the African Brothers, the Fratres Lucis and others of like calibre, were but the outward manifestations of hidden forces which were attempting to indoctrinate the whole Masonic Body with true spiritual, mental and moral Mystic knowledge, because the Masonic body, as such, had already lost the key to its own symbolism and none but the genuine Rosicrucian Fraternity held this key. The leaders of the Order now known as Ancient and Mystic Oriental Masons were Rosicrucians.* Says Findel:—

98. "The Grand Lodge of Germany (The Three

Globes)....'Zu den drei Weltkugeln'....was established by Frederick II., who was its first Grand
Master. It became the Grand Mother Lodge of Germany in 1744. It was also the protectress of the Mystic element in Masonry for many years.'' Cooper-
Oakley further assumes ''that in the Building Fraternities of the Middle Ages, besides their art, a secret
science was carried on; the substratum of which was
a *real* Christian mystery, serving as a preparatory or
elementary school and stepping-stone to that and the
St. John's Masonry, which latter was not a mere system of moral philosophy, but closely allied and connected with this mystery. It was conceded, that the
Freemasonry of our days (St. John's Freemasonry)
sprang from the Building Fraternities of the Middle
Ages, but at the same time asserted that in the early
ages there existed a secret society, which strove to
compass the perfecting of the human race, precisely
in the same manner, and employing similar means,
as did the Swedish system, which, in fact, only followed in the wake of its predecessor, being concealed
in the Building Fraternities, so that our Society did
not rise *from* them, *but made itself a way through
them.* The Secret Science, the Mystery, *was very ancient indeed.* This mystery formed the secret of the
Higher Degrees of the Rite, which *were not merely
kept hidden from the rest of the confederation, but
also from the members of the inferior degrees of the
system itself.* This mystery was fully confirmed by
documents, which the Grand Lodge of Germany had in
its keeping.''

99. This secret legend is the same as that of the Car-
pocratians, which is that Jesus chose some of the
Apostles and confided to them a Secret Science, which
was transmitted afterwards to the priests of the Order
of the Knights Templars, and through them to the
Building Fraternities, down to the present Freemasons
of the Swedish Rite. The Swedish system teaches
that there have been men of *all* nations who have worshipped God in Spirit and in Truth, and surrounded
by idolatry and superstition have yet preserved their
purer faith.

100. Separate from the world, and unknown to it,
this Wisdom has been preserved by them and handed
down as a Mystery.

101. In the time of the Jews they had made use of
the Essenes, in which sect Jesus * was brought up,
and had spent the greater part of His life. Having
been instructed by Him in a more perfect knowledge
of Holy things, they had amidst persecution taught in
Silence that which had been committed to their keeping. At the period of the Saracens and the Crusades
they were so greatly oppressed that they must ultimately have sought for protection from without. As
fate, however, would have it, seven of them, Syriac
Christians, pursued by unbelievers near Bastrum, were
rescued by the Knights Templars, and afterwards
taken under their protection. When they had lived
there for a certain time they begged for permission to

---

*. See both "The Philosophy of Fire" and "The
Rosicrucians; Their Teachings,"

dwell with the Canons or Prebendaries of Jerusalem, as the life there led agreed better with their own inclinations and habits. This was accorded them, and Andreas Montebarrensis effected a union of these Syrians with the Canons, to whom, out of gratitude, they imparted all their science, and so completely did they make the priests of the order the depositories of their secrets that they kept them and handed them over to others under certain conditions.

102. Thus, this secret knowledge, which was continually being added to, lived on in the very heart of the Order of Knights Templars till its abolition. Among these Templars were many Rosicrucians who handed the secret knowledge down from initiate to initiate, and as the Rosicrucian Fraternity has never been abolished from any country, for very good reasons, the secret science has never been disconnected, as it were, as has been the case with every other Order.

103. The clergy were dispersed with the persecution that ensued, but as the secular arm did not touch them as it did the Knights, they managed to rescue many of their secret writings, and when the Knights sought refuge in Scotland, they founded a chapter at Aberdeen, the first Prior of which was Petrus de Bononia. The Science was disseminated from this place, but very cautiously, first to Italy, then to the extreme North (Sweden and Russia) and France. In Italy Abbot Severin had been the guardian of the True Science.

104. "Although it will be acknowledged by every unbiased reader, that Freemasonry has a wonderful resemblance to the Eleusinian and Dionysian Myster-

ies, the fraternity of Ionian architects and the Essenian and Pythagorean * Associations, yet some may be disposed to question the identity of these institutions, because they had different names, and because some usages were observed by one which were neglected by another.

105. But these circumstances of dissimilarity arise from those necessary changes which are superinduced upon every institution, by a spirit of innovation, by the caprice of individuals, and by the various revolutions in civilized society. Every alteration or improvement in philosophical systems, or ceremonial institutions, generally produces a corresponding variation in their name, deduced from the nature of the improvement, or from the name of the innovator.

106. The different associations, for example, whose nature and tendency we have been considering, received their names from circumstances merely casual, and often of trifling consideration; though all of them were established for the same purpose, and derived from the same source. When the mysteries of the Essenes ** were imported by Pythagoras into Italy, without undergoing much variation; they were there denominated the Mysteries of Pythagoras; and, in our own day, they are called the secrets of Freemasonry, because many of their symbols are derived from the art of building, and because they are believed to have been invented by an association of architects, who

---

See ''The Rosicrucians; Their Teachings.''

were anxious to preserve, among themselves, the knowledge which they had acquired."*

107. "The Dionysia, or Mysteries of Bacchus, were intimately connected with those of Ceres and perhaps, still more with Freemasonry; the rites came from Egypt, and there, according to Plutarch Ceres, was the Egyptian Isis, and Bacchus was Osiris.

108. "The Dionysian artificers or architects were an association of scientific men, who were incorporated by command of the Kings of Pergamus into a corporate body, some three hundred years B. C. They had the city of Teos given to them. The members of this association which was intimately connected with the Dionysian mysteries, were distinguished from the uninitiated inhabitants of Teos, by their Science, and by words and signs by which they could recognize their Brethren of the Order. Like Freemasons they were divided into Lodges which were characterized by different names.

109. "Such is the nature of that association of architects, who erected those splendid edifices in Ionia, whose ruins even afford us instructions, while they excite our surprise. If it be possible to prove the identity of any two societies, from the coincidence of their external forms, we are authorized to conclude that the Fraternity of the Ionian architects and the Fraternity of Freemasons, are exactly the same; and as the former practiced the mysteries of Bacchus and Ceres, several of which we have shown to be similar to the mysteries of Masonry, we may safely affirm, that, *in*

* M. Lawrie.

their internal as well as external procedure, the So-
ciety of Freemasons resembles the Dionysians of Asia
Minor.

110. ".We have already shown, from authentic
sources of information, that the mysteries of Ceres
and Bacchus were instituted about four hundred years
before the reign of Solomon,—according to Playfair's
Chronology, the Temple of Solomon was begun in
1016 and finished in 1008 B. C. The Eleusinian My-·
steries were introduced into Athens in 1356, B. C., a
considerable time after their institution........and
there are strong reasons for believing that even the
association of the Dionysian architects existed before
the building of the Temple.

111. "It was not, indeed, till about three hundred
years before the birth of the Christ, that they were
incorporated at Teos, under the Kings of Pergamus;
but it is universally allowed, that they arose long before their settlement in Ionia, and, what is more, to
our present purpose, that they existed in the very land
of Judea.

112. "The difference in the ceremonial observances
of these institutions, may be accounted for nearly upon the same principles. From the ignorance, or superior sagacity of those who presided over the ancient
fraternities, some ceremonies would be insisted upon
more than others, some of less moment would be exalted into consequence, while others of greater importance would be depressed into obscurity. In process of time, therefore, some trifling changes would
be effected upon these ceremonies, some rites abolished,

and some introduced. The Chief difference, however, between the ancient and modern Mysteries, is in those points which concern religion. But this arises from the great changes which have been produced in religious knowledge.

113. "It cannot be supposed that the Rites of the Egyptian, Jewish, and Grecian religions should be observed by those who profess only the religion of Christ; or that we should pour out libations to Ceres and Bacchus, who acknowledge no heavenly superior, but the *true* and the *living* God."*

THE UNDERLYING PRINCIPLE.

114. "The Ancient Wisdom Religion is the 'Thread-soul' on which are strung all the various incarnations and encasements of the religious life, adapted to the changing conditions and developments of humanity in its growth from childhood to manhood.

115. "Begotten by that Spiritual Hierarchy—the Great White Brotherhood—in whose guardianship is the evolution of the human race, brought forth from them, They, the guardians of the Mystic tradition, give to those children of men who are strong enough for the burden, a portion of the *real* teaching of the Divine Science—the Science of the Soul—concerning God and man, and the wonderful relationship that exists between the two.

116. "With the passing of time the old Orders changed, old forms perished, and the Divine Sun that

---

*Alexander Lawrie, "The History of Freemasonry."

shone on the ever-changing screen of time veiled Itself
in new hues, and gathered into new groupings the
humanity of the Western races, and each century
which rolled by, evolved a new phase of the Ancient
Mystic tradition."*

117. "Religious parties, Secret Societies, sects of
every description, such is the shifting panorama of
the Religious life of the world during the last eighteen
hundred years. And as we glance back from our
present standpoint, it is difficult at times to discern
the Mystic traditions, unless one has the Key, so loud
is the clamour of contending sects over their formal
doctrines, the outward expressions of their Inner
faith.

118. "A word may here be said to guard against one
error that might arise with regards to the Spiritual
Hierarchy before mentioned, ** the guardians of the
world's religions. It is from this Great Communion
that the World-Saviours have from time to time come
forth, and from this Center have sprung all the 'Sons
of God,' for there have been many 'Sons of God;' *not
but one,* as some seem to believe.

119. "The building of form—even religious form—
is materializing in its tendency, and thus we see that
in all the centuries subsequent to the inception of

---

*Cooper-Oakley, "Masonry and Mysticism."

**Known as the "Great White Brotherhood" and in
Ancient Mystic Oriental Masonry as the 11th Degree.
Students of the Supreme Initiation will see "The
Beautiful Philosophy of Initiation," by the Count M.
de St. Vincent.

Christianity, the tendency of every 'reformation' has been to throw back, if possible, to the original standard erected by the Founder.''

120. On careful investigation, for instance, we find the Christ responsible only for certain high and pure ideals, insistance being made on a holy life leading to a Divine goal.

The doctrine and elaborations which were *later* introduced arose in *every* case from the followers, who brought in their more *worldly* aims, and *transformed* thereby the *purity* and *simplicity* of the early ideal into an ornate body, with worldly passions and constant strivings for mundane power.

121. ''Hence we find at the end of the nineteenth century, on one side the Catholic Church, on the other the Protestant, *and between the extremes of these doctrinal communities, a fluctuating, ever-increasing body of thinkers, formed by the Mystics and Idealists of both parties, who from century to century have been at variance with their 'orthodox' brethren, seeking a higher truth, a purer ideal, than those offered by the dogmatists.*

122. ''The doctrines hidden in the Secret Fraternities, no matter what the name, have been handed down in regular succession from first to last. We can see that the esoteric teachings which in Atlantis *first*, then in Egypt, in Persia, and in Greece, were kept from the ears of an illiterate multitude precisely because it was known that they could not, in their then uneducated and ignorant condition, understand the deeper truth of Nature and of God. Hence, the secrecy with which

6

these pearls of great price were guarded and handed
on with slight modifications into the possession of those
grand early Christians, the Gnostics, the so-called
heretics; then straight from the Gnostic schools of
Syria and Egypt to their successors, the Manichæans,
and from these through the Paulicians, Albigenses,
and Templars to the Hermetics, the Rosicrucians, and
other less powerful Secret Fraternities—these Occult
traditions, or rather, Occult Truths, have been be-
queathed to the Mystic bodies of our own times. Persecuted by Protestants on one side and by Catholics on
the other, the history of Mysticism, outside of the
Rosicrucian Fraternity, is a history of martyrdom."
123. "These principal streams of religious thought
can be traced distinctly as we struggle through the
labyrinth of evidence, and these may not inappropri-
ately be termed the Petrine, Pauline, and Johannine
doctrines, the last being the fountain-head of all the
later Christian Mystical heresies. The Johannine
doctrine caused great excitement in the fourteenth
century. It must be borne in mind that the *true*
Occultism, the *real* Mysticism, is essentially religious
in its nature, and students must not be surprised to
find that some of the historical religious sects—many
of the principal secret societies take St. John as their
patron saint, notably is this the case with many of the
Masonic bodies—had their foundation in Occultism
and Mysticism before stated, the Occult doctrines of
the Gnostics were heirlooms and sacred traditions from
a very distant past, and when the early Christian era
dawned, the human race had long been plunged in the

darkening and materializing tendencies of the Black
Ages. Soon the Gnosis was rejected by the orthodox
church, and the *Sacred and Secret teachings of the
Great Master, Jesus, became materialized; they have,
however, never been lost, and traces of them can be
discerned from epoch to epoch.*

124. "The Masonic movement, to state it generally,
was at first a sort of broad, semi-mystic and largely
moral movement, worked from certain *unknown,* to
Them, centers, and deriving its *origin from the
Ancient and not generally known basis.*

125. *It never had anything to do with Operative
Masonry or the Builders' Guild. Masonry was
founded on the Ancient Wisdom Religion, and when
founded was not known as Masonry.*

126. Its basis was, and is, unknown to all of those
who do *not* recognize a definitely spiritual guidance in
the practical, mental, and moral developments which
from time to time change the surface by the introduction of new factors into the evolving processes of
which life consists. Researches into Masonic literature
must be made in many languages and countries before
this view can be firmly established for the general
world, but to students of Mysticism and who are also
students of Masonry it becomes more and more apparent that the movement which is generally termed
Masonic had its roots in that *true* Mysticism which
originated, as an Ideal effort, from the Spiritual
Hierarchy which guides the evolution of the world;
and that, however much the branches may be separated
from the root-idea, there is nevertheless a Mystic

teaching in Masonry for those who will seek below the surface.

127. "The Ancients of Atlantis preserved not less than sixteen distinct Secret Orders, all of which constituted—what was known at the time of the advent of Poisedon to the Kingdom of Atlantis—as the Mystic Brother or the Great White Circle. What is now the Fraternity of the Rosy Cross was recognized as the very highest of these Orders, by virtue of their knowledge of the Secret Forces throughout Nature. This Order of men ruled the Destiny of nations and all Institutions.*

128. "With the destruction of Atlantis,** this perfection of order and organization was severed and history from this event only conveys scattering glimpses of these various Orders—all of which, while preserving some remote impressions of their former relationship, have lost trace one of the other."

129. Says John A. Weiss, M.D., in his "Obelisk and Freemasonry:" "According to our reading of history, the *Priesthoods* of Belus, or Baal in Assyria, of Osiris in Egypt, of Jehova in Palestine, of Jupiter in Greece and Rome, of Ahura-Mazda in Persia, or Brahma in India, and of Teutates in Britain, were *Primitive Secret Societies,* who instructed and governed the primitive families and races. It little matters whether we call the members of those priesthoods *Belites, Pastophori, Levites, Curetes, Mage, Brahmins, or Druids;* they were connected by Secret

**See "The Philosophy of Fire."
*See "The Rosicrucians; their Teachings."

Ties, and intercommunicated from the Indus to the Tiber, from the Nile to the Thames. Hence there ever has been, is, and *ever will be* Freemasonry on our planet. Masonry was ever more or less connected with priesthoods till about the thirteenth century of our era, when Masons declared themselves *Freimaurer* (Freemasons). Since about that period priesthoods have ever denounced and persecuted Freemasonry."

130. "A thoughtful consideration of our principal ceremony irresistibly leads us to the doctrine that was typified by the *Pastos* in the King's Chamber of the great Pyramid, and connects with the main characteristic of all the Mysteries, which embodied the highest truths then known to the Illuminated ones.

131. "The twelfth century witnessed an outbreak of Mystic symbolism, perhaps unparalleled, in our era, and gave us the religious legends of the Holy Grail, which point to an Eastern origin; this period coincides with the greatest popularity of the Templars, whose fall is contemporaneous with the decadence noticed by the lecturer.

132. Without pressing the argument, I may suggest that some portion, at least, of our symbolism may have come through a Templar source, Romanist, yet deeply tinged with Gnosticism; while at a later date the Lollards, inheritors of Manichæism, and who were but one of the many religo-political societies with which Europe was honeycombed, possibly introduced or revived some of these teachings. One thing is certain, that satisfactory renderings of our symbols can only be obtained by a study of Eastern Mysticism; Kabal-

6a

istic, Hermetic, Pythagorean and Gnostic.

133. "Down the centuries we find enrolled the names of philosophic teachers who veiled their doctrines in figures similar to those in vogue among the Rosicrucians and still more recent students, and often identical with the signs we blazon on the walls of our Lodges and Chapters: '*Ars Quatuor Coronatorum.* London; 1890.' "

134. "About the year 200 A. D., the most noteworthy Gnostic sect was a Persian branch, the Manichees; it was divided into three classes—Auditors, Elect, and Perfect, and the sect was ruled by twelve Apostles, with a thirteenth as President. Manichæism was always a source of trouble to the Church, and St. Augustine between the years 374 and 383 A. D., was an 'Auditor,' but for some reason could not obtain advancement, and so abandoned the system. The Rite had a Theosophical Gospel which taught that the basis of all religion was one.* In 657 they had changed their name to Paulicians, and later Cathari (The

---

*Says a student under the 11th degree: "The Alchemists and Adepts veil their writings in such a hidden way that it's hard to read between the lines. It is said that Mercury is the *Mystery* of Magic, and that *Mercury is the story of Christ.* It is also the *first* principle of *all* metals. And he who can attract things out of the Mysterium Magnum 'Akasa' is a *true* Alchemist. Also, that this power is possessed only by those who are Spiritually developed.

"It is a marvelous thing to me that the Christ of Orthodoxy, their Crucified Redeemer, etc., is according to Science something so different. As I have been

Purified), Euchites, Bogomiles, and in more recent times still Lollards. We could quote numberless authors of the early period of the Church to prove the origin of these sects from the Eastern Magi, but it is unnecessary and space forbids. In a few words, they were a secret speculative society with degrees, distinguished by signs, tokens and words like Freemasonry, and the Church of Rome from the 4th to the 19th century has hated them with the hatred of death, butchering and burning them by tens of thousands; for Christianity has shed more blood than any other faith. Yet the fathers often admit their purity of life, *but that was their sin against a corrupt priesthood and unpardonable.* The Templars were Gnostics, on the evidence of the Papal trials in 1313, and Hugh, G. M. 1118, is said to have received initiation from Theocletus, Patriarch of St. John the Baptist and the

---

taught (this writer is a Gnostic Initiate) that Akasa is the Hindu Veil for Mercury. I think of Prana and Akasa—Sol and Luna—Sat and Tat—Solar and Lunar principles *ever* working together *as one,* then my thoughts are centered on my heart where, according to Gnostic teachings the Christ of the Mysteries dwells— in the secret chambers of the heart 'Kardiferous Ether,' then again I think of Alchemy and the Sages and wonder about Hermes calling Azot Nitrogen the Virgin of the world, Mercury the Soul of the World. It is said *fire* purifies the dross, Agni is the Mediator. *Call him Mercury or Christ.* And one must seek this Christ *within*—which is called a *Mystic Fire.* The heart is called the seat of Life where the sixth Ether Cardiferous, the Christ of the Mystics dwells. 'The Sixth Tattia is Soul Knowledge.' "

Codex Nazareus.''*

135. ''The days of Constantine were the last turn-ing point in history. The period of the Supreme struggle that ended in the Western world throttling the old religion in favor of the new ones, built on their bodies. From thence the vista into the far distant Past, beyond the 'Deluge' and the 'Garden of Eden,' began to be forcibly and relentlessly closed by every fair and unfair means against the indiscreet gaze of Posterity. Every issue was blocked up, every record that hands could be laid upon, destroyed.

136. ''This *same* Constantine who, with his soldiers environed the Bishops at the first Council of Nice, A. D. 325, and dictated terms to their deliberations, ap-plied *for Initiation into the Mysteries, and was told by the Officiating Priest that no purgation could free him from the crime of putting his wife to death, or from his many purjuries and murders*. Every careful and unbiased student of history knows why the Secret Doctrine has been heard of so little since the days of Constantine. An exoteric religion, and belief in a personal God blotted it out for self protection; and yet, oh, irony of history! the very Pentateuch conceals it, and for many a student of the Kabalah of the coming century, the seals will be broken.''* *

137. ''Three centuries had passed since the orgin of Christianity when at this epoch of barbarism there arose in the same Persia, whence so many teachings

*John Yarker, ''Records and Documents of Free-masonry.''

* *Dr. J. D. Buck, ''Mystic Masonry.''

had gone forth, a philosopher who wished to lead back the confused spirit of men to the cult of *the only true* God. He was called Manes. Some of the uninstructed have regarded him as the first originator of our (Masonic) Order, and the creator of our doctrines.

138. "Manes lived under the Persian King Sopares. He endeavored to recall to life in their entire *purity* the Mysteries and the religion of Zoroaster, uniting them with the *pure compassionate teachings of* Jesus Christ. The Teachings of Manes were liberal, whereas superstition and despotism governed Europe. It is easy to believe that those who professed demagogic principles and a religion free from all that was chimerical would be persecuted. Thus the Manichæans from about the fourth century were persecuted to the fullest by all the despots and by the Romish Priests. The Holy Augustine, brought up in the mysteries of Zoroaster—to a certain point—adapted to the holy teachings of Jesus, became his bitterest persecutor and the greatest enemy to the teachings of Manes which was known under the name of the *religion of the Child of the Widow.*

139. "This hatred shown towards Manes by St. Augustine, and his zeal to the Christian Trinity doctrine—after he had been refused admittance to the Higher Degrees of the Mysteries—arose in the vexation which Augustine experienced at having been only admitted into the first degree of the Mysteries of Manes. The Magi, who had recognized in him an ambitious and restless spirit, were thereby induced to refuse to him all advancement, and this in spite of his nine years

study, which he made in order to be raised to the higher degree. This fact is sufficiently confirmed by Fleury, Baronius, and by Augustine himself in his confessions. After the death of Manes, twelve of his pupils went forth into all the parts of the earth and imparted his teachings and his mysteries to all people. They illumined, as with a lightning-flash, Asia, Africa, and Europe, as may be seen from Baronius, Fleury, Bayle, and others.

140. "Already in the lifetime of Manes, his pupil Herman had spread his teachings in Egypt, where Coptic priests and other Christians mingled it with the mysteries adopted from the Jews. It was through these same Coptic priests and the Eastern Christians that both the mysteries of the Children of the Widow, and the cult of the great Architect came to us in consequence of apparently unforseen events, and it will be seen that it was principally by means of the Crusades that they obtained a secure footing in the West. The mysteries maintained their existence under the name of the cult of the Great Architect of the Universe (G. A. O. T. U.), a name that has its origin in the allegory of Hiram, which represented, in the Mysteries, 'The unknown God,' the Eternal, and sole Creator of *all* things and the Regenerator of all beings.

141. "Bossuet, in his *Historie des Variations, IV,* says that in the middle ages the Christian sects, and especially the Manichæans and Gnostics, had concealed themselves as much as possible in the Orthodox Church itself; the remainder of the Manichæans who had

maintained themselves only too well in the East, crowded into the Latin Church. Montfaucon, VII, p. 271, says, when he speaks of the religion of the Egyptians, that the heresy of the good and evil principles which had been upheld by Manichæans, had at various times brought forth in the Church great disorder, and he asserts that in the East........these doctrines existed at the time of the Crusades......... the long time that elapsed during the wars of the Crusaders gave them the opportunity of being admitted into all the mysteries of the Children of the Widow, the teachings of the 'Great Architect of the World,' and of both principles......the Crusaders who had been admitted to the mysteries of the Children of the Widow and initiated therein, imparted them, on their return home, to their pupils in Europe...... during the sojourn of the Crusaders with the Mussulmans, all kinds of theological investigations were instituted. These led the Crusaders deeper into the faith in the Great Architect of the World (G. A. O. T. W.).

142. "In spite of the religious changes that followed upon the conquests of the Saracens in Asia, and Europe; in spite of the persecutions introduced by them, the doctrines as to the Unity of God was able to maintain itself by means of the Mysteries in Palestine, Syria, and Egypt, more especially, however, in the neighborhood of Thebes; for here the Christians and Coptic priests preserved, in the lap of their solitude, the teachings communicated to them by Herman, the pupil of Manes, a teaching which later passed over

into Europe.''*

143. "It is proved that the Emperor Rudolph I, even in the year 1275, authorized an Order of Masons, whilst Pope Nicholas III, in the year 1278, granted to the Brotherhood of Stonemasons at Strausburg, a letter of Indulgence, which was renewed by all his successors down to Benedict XII, in 1340. The oldest order of German Masons arises in the year 1397; next follow the so-called Vienna Witnesses of 1412, 1430, and 1435; then the Strassburg Order of Lodges, 1495; that of Torgau of 1462, and finally sixteen different Orders on to 1500, and to the following centuries for Spires, Regensburg, Saxon-Altenburg, Strassburg, Vienna, and the Tyrol.''**

144. "At this period the Roman Church appears to have made various futile efforts to retain a hold upon these Masons, but without tangible results. For the forces at the back of these movements prevented the destruction of a new free spiritual growth by the Roman power. At this period also came those great souls, burning for freedom, who worked the Reformation, such as John Tauler, the famous Dominican, who formed a Mystical Fraternity, the members of which recognized each other by secret signs. Then we have Nicholas of Basle, with his four disciples, the beginning of the 'Friends of God.' These men kept watch on all that was going on in the world, and they had special messengers who had certain secret signs, by

*Reghellini da Schio, Paris, 1883.
**Ludwig Abafi, "Pre-Historic Freemasonry in Australia, etc."

which they recognized each other; Nicholas was burned as a heretic. Although these reforms were dwarfed of their full growth by the natural crudity and narrow-ness of the human mind, nevertheless the dogmatic and mind-killing power of Rome was materially thwarted, and the spirit in the teachings of the Master Christ set free from those trammels. Writes Abafi:

145. "Equally important in the formation of Free-masonry were certain religious communities and brotherhoods of the Middle Ages, which for the most part aimed at a return to the *pure* teachings of Christ, and at making its ethical form familiar to their ad-herents. One of these brotherhoods was that of the Waldenses, established by Peter Waldo in the year 1170, at Lyons. Their aim was the restitution of the original purity of the Church through the adoption of voluntary poverty, and the other ascetic practices. But because of the doctrine of Transubstantiation they soon came into conflict with the Catholic Church, and as early as 1134, Pope Lucias III excommunicated them, and Sextus IV, in 1477, proclaimed a Crusade against them. In spite of these attacks they have kept alive up to the present day, and have spread into several countries, namely, into Italy, France and Bo-hemia, and in this latter country we shall meet them again under the name 'Bohemian Brothers.'

146. "A few words may be summarized from the same writer about some of the other Mystic bodies in Bohemia and Hungary, lands full of Occult tendencies. Among them are the following: 'Die Bruder von Reif und Hammer,' or the 'Brothers of the Circle and

Hammer,' 'Die Hackebrudershaft,' or 'The Brotherhood of the Hatchet,' 'Die Freunde vom Kreuz,' or
the 'Friends of the Cross.' This last society spread
into the Netherlands, and had its greatest success in
the latter part of the 17th Century. The 'Brothers of
the Cross' were still holding their meetings in 1785;
they had many members in Wallachia, and still more
in Transylvania. Brabbee, in his Masonic studies,
says: 'It consisted principally of *Older men and
those who were generally reputed wise, and therefore
of the prominent leaders of the Brotherhood, who here,
in the Metropolis of the Kingdom, formed a kind of
stronghold on the "Inner East."* ' "

147. "The last expression (in italics) is worthy of
our notice, for it shows how the minds of men were
turning, even in Masonic Circles, to the Eastern teachings. Abafi also says that a great and moulding force
was exercised at this period on the form of Freemasonry by Jan Amos Kemensky (latinized Comenius),
who was born at Brunn, in Bohemia, in 1592, and who
became a chaplain of the Bohemian Brothers in 1618.
When the civil wars began Komensky lost wife, child,
and property, and was exiled from Austria like all
other non-Catholics. He escaped to Poland, turned
his thoughts to educational matters, and became
famous in Sweden, Hungary, and England.

148. "Komensky was actively interested in the
Rosicrucian movement, and joined John Valentinus
Andreas, the reformer of the Rosicrucian Fraternity,*

*See "The Fraternity of the Rosicrucians; their
Teachings."

in his work in that body. In 1650 Komensky was invited to Hungary and Transylvania by the Prince Ragozcy, where he stayed four years. It is doubtless partly owing to his influence that the Rosicrucian movement spread so widely in these countries. His philosophical and metaphysical views were so widely spread, that when Anderson wrote his book on Freemasonry, he, according to Abafi, incorporated in his work a compilation of the most essential portions of the plans of Komensky."

149. Says Abafi: "It was reserved for an Austrian, a Moravian school-master, the Chaplain of the Bohemian Brothers, to bestow ethical treasures upon a brotherhood in proud Albion, the home of the boldest intellects; to formulate the ideas, and to point out the way for a league which—after its transformation—was destined to embrace the noblest of all nations, and being brought to perfection by them, ordained to influence the whole of humanity."

149½. "The spread of Mysticism in Austria and Hungary during the last century was astoundingly rapid; according to von Andrée, about five per cent. of the entire population belonged to the Freemasons, Rosicrucians, and other allied societies."

150. "In a German tract, printed about 1803, and bound up with another tract called 'Geschichte der Freimaurerei,' occur the following statements, which the true Masonic student will find very valuable and which show, as does all literature of any value, that the Rosicrucians were the *real* heads of *all* Masonic bodies.

1. "The Templars worked with the so-called 'Magical Brethren' at an early period of their existence.

2. "A Rosicrucian manuscript states that at Cologne, with the motto, '*non Omnis Moriar,*' this Magical Union was created there in 1115.

3. "A manuscript of Michael Mayer's still exists in the University Library at Leyden, which sets forth that in 1570 the society of the old Magical Brethren, or 'Wise Men,' was revived under the name of Brethren of the Golden Rosy Cross.

4. "It is asserted that in 1563 the Statutes of the Brotherhood were, on the 22d of September, at Basle, at a meeting of seventy-two Masters of Lodges, revised, set forth, and printed; that the Lodges of Swabia, Hesse, Bavaria, Franconia, Saxony, Thuringia, and those on the Moselle acknowledged the headship of the Grand Lodge of Strassburg. That in the eighteenth century Lodges of Dresden and Nuremberg were fined by the Grand Master of Strasburg, and that the Grand Lodge of Vienna, or Hungary, and Stirrmark, the Grand Lodge of Zurich, which ruled the Swiss Lodges, referred to the Mother Lodge of Strassburg in all difficult and doubtful matters."

151. Says a student: "There can be no doubt that the Theosophical and Magical Union above mentioned did exist as an organized Secret Society. The correspondence of Cornelius Agrippa von Nettersheim shows that he was a member of such a Secret Society ('Militia Crucifera Evangelica'), and it is further asserted that when he was in London he established a

branch of it in that city. Fludd (the Rosicrucian), as showing that secret societies existed in the Universities, has the passage 'notwithstanding any allegiance which I may have vowed by a ceremonial Rite to Aristotle (the Gnostic principles were spread under the form of Aristotelean Philosophy at Paris and elsewhere) in my youth. These societies used the double Triangles, or Seal of Solomon, and in the ruins of one of the old Temple Preceptories in France was found a copper medallion with the Lamb surmounted by this Cabalistic symbol.' "

152. "Two points," writes Cooper-Oakley, "in this interesting note can be corroborated by further evidence. The Rosicrucian manuscript mentioned in paragraph 2 is also mentioned on page 56 of a most valuable German book by Friedrich Gottlieb Ephraim Weisse, or Magister Pianco; it is called *Der Rosenkreutzer in seiner Blosse*, (Amsterdam, 1781). Some extracts from it will not be without interest, for it refers to the other body of 'Wise-Men,' who were known as the 'Unknown Heads' of many of the small societies. The conditions of entrance are briefly given, as follows:

3. " 'Whosoever wished to be admitted to the secrets, and afterwards to be initiated, must be a man of honour and of true spiritual power; and he must be already of considerable learning; for only those were accepted, of whom it could be hoped that they would be of great service to the Sacred Alliance.

10. " 'The Initiates wore a triangle, symbolical of

7

the three qualities of the Dumiurgos—Power, Wisdom and Love.

"'The Masters of the second degree or Second Secret, were Masters in the knowledge of all nature, and her forces and divisions.

11. "'They were called Philosophers or the World Wise (now Rosicrucians). Their science was called the World-Wisdom.

12. "'These World-Wise occupied themselves in secret. No one knew where they met, or what they did.

14. "'But they had also secret sciences known only to the highest among them—called Magos, Mage, or the Wise Master, who taught the people Divine things.'"

153. "Those Brother Masons (of the highest degrees) knew that they owed their brotherhood to the Initiations of the old Wise-Men (Rosicrucians); that the great part of their (the Masons') knowledge came from Them, and that without Their help they could do nothing."

154. "Long before the year 1118, there was a Society which in the mysteries of the ancients took the place of the last and youngest grade, and which had the same position with the Tempelherren, who had adopted it with the other teachings of the Wise Ones. They were the novices from all times. As in the time of the Inquisition against the Templars no one knew anything about the lower and last grades, and those who belonged to them had no public connection with them and thus lived without attracting any attention, they were overlooked in the cruelties of the time. One

did not think of them. As the members of the
Templars who escaped were few in number and died
one after the other, the remaining members drew together to form a bond of friendship, to which end they
drew up certain rules. This new society appeared in
different forms and under different names, Cross
Society or Brothers of the Cross, Noaities, and in later
days adopted the name of Freemasons.

155. "Length of time and the involved issues consequent thereon made those initiated into the Mysteries
at length perceive that they must introduce an entirely different organization into the community, in
order to bring it into line with Christianity.

156. "Those associates who still remained over
from the collapse (the 'Magian Brothers,' who followed Manes, the Reformer,) of the community of
Initiates, and who were scattered about the world,
began to make fresh projects for a general union.
They took the laws of their community and the laws
of the Christians, which are known under the name of
the Bible, into a real assimilation. They began to
institute a parallel between the books of Moses and
the memorials of the Magi, and from all this they
evolved a kind of association, provided with certain
laws, which could fit in with the Christians.

157. "The association was, as is always the custom
with innovations, in the beginning somewhat dark and
involved; it was saddled with various meanings and
names, which it would be useless to repeat here, but
which were all of short duration, so that the first ones
called it the association of Magi and its members the

Magi Brotherhood and associates. And this first association was formed in the year 1115 and lasted till the year 1117, though it underwent changes from time to time. The Crusaders had given rise to many societies and orders amongst the profane, and associations had sprung up which had quite differing objects.''*

158. Says Baron Hans Ecker von Eckhoffen, in his treatise, when writing of the Asiatische Brueder: ''These writings date from 1510; showing that a body of Mystics was known at that period; these Knights of Asia also called themselves the Knights of St. John, and it is a curious fact to notice that one of the Masonic records which has caused an infinity of discussion, and also of dissension, amongst Masons, is the celebrated 'Cologne Record,' which is dated 1535, and in which an Order of St. John is noticed. This Charter has been a veritable bone of contention between materialistic and Mystic Masons, and much polemical literature has been published on the subject. The Mystics hold (and rightly so) it to be true on external and internal evidences; while the materialists reject it, as they reject all such evidence.

159. ''In the record there is the name of Philip Melancthon—the friend and co-worker of Martin Luther—who appears as a Brother in the Order of Freemasons. This document bears witness also that a secret society was known in various parts of the world, which existed before 1440 under the name of the 'Brotherhood of St. John,' and since then, and up to

*Op. Cit.

1535, under the title, the 'St. John's Order of Free-masonry,' or 'Masonic Brotherhood.'

160. "This Society (the present Masonic body) was reformed and re-arranged in the year 1717, the gener-ally accepted modern date of the Materialistic and non-mystic Masons. It became more atheistic in its views, and more democratic in its tendencies.

161. "Amongst other deeply interesting matter, the 'Charter of Cologne' contains the following passage:

162. " 'The Brotherhood, or the order of Freemason Brothers, bound together according to St. John's Holy rules, traces its origin neither from the Templars nor from any other spiritual or temporal Knightly Order, but it is older than all similar Orders, and has existed in Palestine and Greece, as well as in various parts of the Roman Empire. Before the Crusades our Brother-hood arose; at a time when in consequence of the strife between the sects teaching Christian morals, a small number of the initiated—entrusted with the true teaching of virtue, and the sensible exposition of the secret teaching—separated themselves from the mass.'

163. "According to the record, the following reason was given for the adoption of the name: The Masters of this confederation were called the St. John's Brethren, as they had chosen John the Baptist, the forerunner of the Light of the World, as their original and example."

164. "It is well to add here a few details about the Knights Templars, since they are so intimately con-nected with the Masonic Order; details which will

7a

serve to show the inner aspect of their traditions.
Much has been written about them and their history—
from one aspect—is better known than that of almost
any other Mystic organization, but the fact of a secret
teaching is not sufficiently clear. That there was a
secret doctrine amongst the Templars is shown by
Neaf, in his '*Recherches sur les Opinions religieuses
des Templliers.*' He points out that the Knights considered that the Roman Church had failed in its ideal,
and that when the terrible persecutions fell upon
them that they divided and joined two different associations, one the body of Freemasons and the other a
body named the Johannites. Another writer, Jules
Loiseleur, points out the connection between the
Templars and the Bogomiles, who were the Manichæans of the Balkan Provinces, and the Gnostics of
the early Christian period and their descendants, the
Cathari of the mediaeval ages. Dr. Simrock, in his
work, suggests a deeply interesting idea with regard
to the connection between the tradition of the Holy
Grail and the secret teachings of the Templars; he
considers that the Grail tradition, which is drawn in
some parts from the Apocryphal Gospels, is the basis
of the Secret Teachings of the Templars. Some of the
early sources of the tradition are given by the author
of Sarsena, and also the connection between the
Templars and the Essenes (Rosicrucians).

165. All these links are of importance if we wish to
understand the close connection between these various
organizations, and also how one developed out of the
other.

166. "Taking the rules of their Order and of the Christians in equal division, they (the Kabalists) began to draw a parallel between the books of Moses and the records of the Magi, and formed from all this material a new Brotherhood into which they imported certain rules that could exist together with those of the .Christians. During the Crusades there were several orders of widely different views; and among numerous others in the year 1118, the Knights of the Temple, with whom the Magi joined themselves, and to whom they imparted their principles and mysteries. The fall of the Templars and the entire demolition of the Order by the Council held in Vienna in 1311, is due to the fact that all the knowledge which we may consider as part of the Wisdom of the ancient Magi, and also the Natural Sciences, had at this time begun to be lost. There is one section of Freemasons which finds in Freemasony the restoration of the Order of the Knights Templars, and the systems of the Great German Lodge and that of the Swedish Brothers are certainly pre-eminently connected with the former. According to this system, and in especial according to all the various systems which obtain in this par-ticular Order, Freemasonry is a Mystical conception of the principal doctrines of Christianity, the slain Master no other than the Christ! And here the question fairly arises, had the teachings of the Christ in truth Mysteries, unsearchable, incomprehensible doc-trines, which were only to be made comprehensible to a small number of especially chosen disciples, and were not the Essenes (the Rosicrucians) that body

among whom He had learned those Mysteries?* For
the Essenes (Rosicrucians) demanded of those initiated, moderation, justice, avoidance of injury, love
of Truth and detestation of evil; holy water belonged
to the Ritual of admission to their highest grade, and
John said 'Repent and be baptized.' Christ, who led
the blameless life, suffered himself to be baptized.
Does not this lead us to the almost certain conclusion
that Christ, and even more John, were initiated
members of the Essenes?** Were sufficient documents available to prove the historic truth of this
statement, it would be perfectly obvious why John
(the Baptist), who bled for Truth and Goodness,
should have been chosen as the Patron of the present
Order and of nearly all that precede it. The keeping
of John the Baptist's Day as a Festival by the Freemasons is adduced in confirmation of this idea that
the Freemasons had for over six hundred years identified themselves with the 'Johannrittern,' and St. John
the Baptist had been chosen Patron of both Orders.
And as it is certain that much of the ritual of the
form of Reception means something quite other than
that which has been substituted latterly, it may very
easily be that there is some truth in this assertion.
For it is just as little true that the Freemasons identified themselves six hundred years ago with the
'Johannrittern' as that they now crown the Master,
Hiram, in the Lodge in *real* earnest. Christ, as has
been said above, founded no secret society, and yet He

*See "The Philosophy of Fire."
**See "The Philosophy of Fire."

gave out His teachings *only* by degrees as regard its *inner* Significance, for He said, 'I have many things to say unto you, but ye cannot bear them now.' After His death the pure doctrine was falsified by additions, but yet it.may be possible that its pristine purity and simplicity may have been preserved, and where else than in some kind of Order? In the early Christian Church there was a *disciplina arcani*, and in this manner were the Mysteries transmitted among the few, and even in the time of the Crusades there were still living descendants of the Essenes. The Order of Knights of the Temple was founded in the year 1113 by Gottfried von St. Omar, Hugo de Paiens, and seven others whose names are not known. They consecrated themselves to the service of God according to the form of the *Canonicorum Regularium,* and took solemn vows before the Bishop of Jerusalem. Baldwin the Second, in consideration of the office of these seven servants of God, lent them a house near the Temple of Solomon. They bound themselves with certain Essenes (Rosicrucians) who formed a secret society consisting of virtuous Christians and true seekers after Truth in Nature, and learned also their secrets. That the Templars had Mysteries in their keeping is beyond contention. The Order had secret ceremonies of admission, glorified in possessing such, and for this reason several of its members endured martyrdom. The Order of Knights Templars contained many of the best and most far-seeing minds among the parents of Freemasonry; and, as is well known, there were whole branches of Freemasonry specially devoted to the restoration of the Templars. And the Johannine and other systems taught this descent, even before the 'Strict Observance' became generally known, which insisted on the restoration of the Templars as the highest aim of the Mysteries. If we consider closely the similarity between the customs of both Orders we shall find that the Reception and other ceremonies of the Order of Freemasonry relates to that of the Knights of the Temple exactly in so far as to enable us to say with positiveness that the Freemasons preserve in their midst the Mysteries of the Templars and transmit them. That the Templars possessed secrets is witnessed by the evidence in their procedure: the Fremasons claim the like procedure for themselves, for from grade to grade the Aspirant is told that later he shall experience yet more. More what? Also a secret. Nine Brothers founded the Order of the Templars; the chief and hieroglyphic number of the Freemasons in three times three. The Templars held Divine Service in places which were interdicted. By the strictest observances they reserved these for themselves (or set these aside), they appealed to the rights of their forefathers.''

167. ''The Brother Templars,'' says Roessler, ''were, according to their statutes as Hospital Brothers, divided into three classes: 1, into the class of the serving, who, without distinction, nursed sick pilgrims and Knights Templars; 2, into that of the spiritual Brothers destined for the service of pilgrims; 3, into that of Knights who went to war.

168. ''We find in the Instructions of the Chevalier

d'Orient, where are celebrated the foundation of the Knights Templars and the spread of their teachings in Europe, the following declaration on the matter is given:

169. "Eighty-one Masons under the leadership of Garimonts, the Patriarch of Jerusalem, went, in the year 1150, to Europe and betook themselves to the Bishop of Upsala, who received them in very friendly fashion and was consequently initiated into the mysteries of the Copts which the Masons had brought with them; later he was entrusted with the deposit of the collection of those teachings, rites and mysteries. The Bishop took pains to enclose and conceal them in the subterranean vaults of the tower of the 'Four Crowns,' which at that time was the crown treasure chamber of the King of Sweden. Nine of these Masons, amongst them Hugo de Paganis, founded in Europe the Order of the Knights Templars; later on they received from the Bishop the dogmas, mysteries and teachings of the Coptic Priests, confided to him.

170. "Thus in a short time the Knights Templars became the receivers and depositors of the Mysteries, Rites and Ceremonies which had been brought over by the Masons from the East—the Levites of the *true* Light.

171. "The Knights Templars, devoted entirely to the sciences and to the dogmas brought from the Thebaid, wished, in course of time, to preserve this doctrine in solemn fashion by a token. The Scotch Templars served as pattern in the matter, they having founded the three degrees of St. Andreas of Scotland,

and adapted them to the allegorical legend to be found
in the instructions referred to.

172. "Scotch Templars were occupied in excavating
a place at Jerusalem in order to build a temple there,
and precisely on the spot where the temple of Solomon—or at least that part of it called the Holy of
Holies—had stood. During their work they found
three stones which were the cornerstones of the Solomon temple itself. The monumental form of these
excited their attention; this excitement became all the
more intense when they found the name of Jehovah
engraved in the elliptical spaces of the last of these
stones—this which was also a type of the Mysteries of
the Copt—the sacred word which, by the murder of
the Master Builder, had been lost, and which, according to the legend of the first degree, Hiram had had
engraved on the foundation-stone of Solomon's
Temple. After such a discovery the Scotch Knights
took this costly memorial with them, and, in order
eternally to preserve their esteem for it, they employed
these as the three cornerstones of the first temple at
Edinburg.

173. "The works began on St. Andreas' day; and
so the Templars who had knowledge of this fact, of
the secret of the three stones, and of the re-discovered
word, called themselves Knights of St. Andreas; they
appointed degrees of merit in order to attain, and
these are present in the Apprentice, Fellow Craft, and
Master degrees, known under the name of the Little
Master-Builder, the Great Master-Builder and the
Scotch Master.

174. "By the instruction common to all Knightly Orders the Crusaders were under obligation to make many journeys and pilgrimages where, as is said, they had to see themselves surrounded by dangers. Therefore, they founded those degrees in order to recognize each other and to assist each other in need. For these journeys they took signs, words, and particular touches or grips, and imparted to all Brothers a principal sign in order to find help in case of a surprise.

175. "In order to imitate the Christians of the East and the Coptic Priests, these Knights Preserved among themselves the verbal law which was never written down, and took care that it should remain concealed to the initiated of the lower degrees. All this is preserved with exactitude in the philosophic rite of our days, although this rite does not precisely seek to derive its origin from the Knights Templars.

176. "The Knights Templars united the possessions of the Old Man of the Mountains under their rule, as they had perceived the supernatural courage of his pupils, they admitted these into their order. Some historians have thus come to the opinion that the Knights Templars had been induced themselves to accept the institutions of those admitted. Gauthier von Montbar was acquainted with these teachings, and transplanted them into Europe.

177. "All these circumstances were very detrimental to the religion of Rome; it lost many of those who had belonged to it; more especially many Cru-

saders who were sojourning in Syria, Palestine and
Egypt, where all the forms of belief of the first
Christians were preserved and tolerated by the
Saracens.

178. "Eastern Christians regarded the dogma of
the unity of God as a mystery and saw in it a Divine
manifestation. They, therefore, only imparted the
knowledge thereof at initiation which they held very
secret. They practiced the morality commanded by
the Son of Mary, but did not believe in his divinity;
for all those who followed Gnostic and Kabalistic
traditions considered him to be their Elder Brother.

179. "The Knights of the Cross who had come to
know these dogmas and mysteries of the Christians
of the East, were obliged, when they had returned to
Europe, to hold this initiation still more secret, for
the mere suspicion of such a faith would have been
sufficient to bring these new religious professors to
the rack and the stake."

180. As regarding to the link between the Knights
Templars and the Gnostic teachings (the Masonic
"G" *does not and never did, stand for Geometry, but
for "Gnosis," the soul*) it is well to quote from Abbe
Gregoire when he says:

181. "The Order of the Temple is cosmopolitan; it
is divided into two great classes: 1, the Order of the
East; 2, the Order of the Temple.

182. "The Order of the Temple sprang from the
Order of the East, of which Ancient Egypt was the

cradle. The Order of the East comprised different orders or classes of adepts. The adepts of the first order were at once legislators, judges, and pontiffs.

183. "Their policy was opposed to the propagation of metaphysical knowledge and the natural sciences, of which they made themselves the sole depositories; and whoever should have dared to reveal the secrets reserved for the initiates in the order of the sacerdotal hierarchy, would have been punished with most dire severity. They gave to the people only unintelligible emblems constituting the exoteric theology, which was a compound of absurd dogmas and extravagant practices tending to give more ascendency to superstition, and to consolidate the government.

184. "Moses was initiated in Egypt. He was profoundly versed in the theological, physical, and metaphysical mysteries of the priests. Aaron, his brother, and the other Hebrew chiefs became the depositories of these doctrines. These chiefs, or Levites, were divided into several classes, according to the custom of the Egyptian priests.

185. "Later on, the Son of God was born into the world. He was brought up in the Alexandrian school. Filled with a spirit altogether Divine, endowed with the most marvelous intelligence, He succeeded in attaining *all the degrees of the Egyptian (Essenian)* Initiation.

186. "On returning to Jerusalem, he presented himself before the chiefs of the Synagogue, and

pointed out to them the numerous alterations that the Law of Moses had undergone at the hands of the Levites; he confounded them by the power of His spirit and the extent of his knowledge; but the Jewish priests, blinded by their passions, persisted in their errors.

187. "However, the moment had come when the Christ, directing the fruits of His lofty meditations towards the universal civilization and welfare of the world, tore down the veil which hid the truth from the people, preached the love of one's neighbor and the equality of all men before the common Father. Finally, consecrating by a sacrifice worthy of the Son of God the heavenly doctrines which He had come to spread, He established forever on the earth, by His gospels, the religion inscribed in the Book of Eternity.

188. "Jesus conferred on His disciples the evangelical Initiation, caused His spirit to descend upon them, divided them into different orders, according to the custom of the Egyptian priests and Hebrew priests, and placed them under the authority of St. John, his beloved disciple, and whom He had made Supreme pontiff and patriarch.

189. "John never quitted the East; his doctrine, always pure, was not altered by the admixture of any other doctrine.

190. "Peter and the other apostles, on the contrary, carried the teachings of Christ to distant peoples; but as they were often forced, in order to

propagate the faith, to conform to the manners and customs of these different nations, and even to admit other rites than those of the East, slight variations and changes crept into the different gospels, as well as into the doctrines of the numerous Christian sects.

192. "Down to 1118, the Mysteries and the hierarchical order of the Egyptian Initiation, transmitted to the Jews through Moses and afterwards to the Christians through Jesus Christ, were religiously preserved by the successors of the apostle John. These mysteries and these initiations regenerated through the evangelical initiation or baptism formed a sacred deposit which, thanks to the simplicity of primitive customs from which the brothers of the East never departed, never underwent the slightest alteration.

193. "The Christians of the East, persecuted by the infidels, appreciating the courage and piety of those valiant crusaders who, sword in one hand and cross in the other, flew to the defence of the holy places; doing justice, above all, to the virtues and the ardent charity of Hugh of Payens, considered it their duty to entrust to hands so pure the treasures of knowledge acquired during so many centuries, and sanctified by the cross, the teachings and the ethics of the Man-God.

194. "Hugh was then invested with the patriarchal apostolic power, and placed in the legitimate line of the successors of John the Apostle or Evangelist.

195. "Such is the origin of the foundation of the

8

Templars, and of the introduction amongst them of the different modes of initiation of the Christians of the East designated by the name of Primitive or Johannite Christians. It is to this initiation that belong the various degrees consecrated by the rules of the Temple, and which were so much called in question in the famous but terrible action brought against this august Order.

196. ''Jacques de Molay, foreseeing the misfortunes that threatened the Order, appointed as his successor Brother Jean Marc Larmenius, of Jerusalem, and with magisterial power.

197. ''This Grand Master passed on the supreme power to Brother Theobald, of Alexandria, as is evidenced by the character of transmission, etc. ,

198. ''Let us come finally to the Levitical doctrines: God is all that exists; every part of all that exists is a part of God, but is not God.

199. ''Immutable in His essence, God is mutable in His parts, which after having existed under the laws of certain combinations more or less complex, live again under laws of fresh combinations. All is increate.

200. ''God being supremely intelligent, every one of the parts which compose Him is endowed with a portion of His intelligence, in virtue of its destiny, whence it follows that there is an infinite gradation of intelligence resulting from an infinity of different compounds, the union of which forms the entirety of

the worlds. This entirety is the Great All, or God, who alone has the power to modify, change, and govern all these orders of intelligences according to the eternal and immutable laws of an infinite justice and goodness.

201. "God—infinite Being—is composed of three powers; the Father, or Being; the Son, or action; the Spirit, or mind, proceeding from the power of the Father and the Son. These three powers form a trinity, a power infinite, unique and individual.

202. "There is but one only *true* religion, that which acknowledges one only God, Eternal, filling the infinity of time and space.

203. "The Order of Nature is immutable; therefore all doctrines that any one would attempt to build up on a change of these laws would be founded only on error.

204. "Eternal life is the power with which every being is endowed, of living in his own life and of acquiring an infinity of modifications by combining himself unceasingly with other beings, according to what is ordained by the eternal laws of the wisdom, the justice and the infinite goodness of the supreme Intelligence.

205. "According to this system of modification of matter, it is natural to conclude that all its parts have the right of thought and free-will, and therefore the power of merit and demerit; hence there is no longer anything of what is called inorganic matter; if,

however, any must be admitted, where is the limit, for instance, among minerals, vegetable, and animal substances?

206. "However, the high Initiates do not profess to believe that all the parts of matter possess the faculty of thought. It is not thus that they profess to understand their system. They certainly admit a series of intelligences from the elementary substance, the most simple molecule, or the monad, up to the reunion of all these monads or of their compounds, a reunion which would constitute the great All, or God, which, as the Universal Intelligence, would alone have the power of comprehending Itself. But the manner of being, of feeling, and of using the intelligence, would be relative to the hierarchical order in which they found themselves placed; consequently the intelligence would differ according to the mode of organization and the hierarchical place of each body. Thus, according to this system, the intelligence of the simple molecule would be limited to seeking or rejecting union with certain other molecules. The intelligence of a body composed of several molecules would have other characters, according to the mode of organization of its elements, and the higher or lower degree that it occupied in the hierarchical scale of compounds. Man, for example, among the intelligences which form part of the earth, would alone have that modification or organization which would fully give the "I" consciousness, as well as the faculty of *distinguishing* good from evil, and consequently which would procure the gift of free-will."

MASONIC SYMBOLISM

AND THE

ANCIENT MYSTERIES ALL ARE ONE

207. "The Order known as Freemasonry appears to have been instituted as a vehicle to preserve and transmit an account of the miraculous dealings of the Most High with His people in the infancy of the world; for at that early period Freemasonry may be identified with religion.

208. "The identity of the Masonic Institution with the Ancient Mysteries is obvious from the striking coincidences found to exist between them. The latter was a secret religious worship, and the depository of religion, science and art. Tradition dates the origin of the Mysteries back to the earliest period of time, and makes it coeval with the organization of Society.

209. "But the order of Freemasonry goes further than did the Ancient Mysteries; while it embodies all that is valuable in the institutions of the past, it embraces within its circle all that is good and true of the present, and thus becomes a *conservator* as well as a *depository* of religion, science and art.

8a

210. "Without any reference to forms and modes of faith, it furnishes a series of indirect evidences, which silently operate to establish the great and general principles of religion, and points to that triumphant system which was the object of all preceding dispensations, and must ultimately be the sole religion of the human race, because it is the only religion in which the plan of salvation is clearly developed."[*]

211. "From age to age, through countless generations, these Rites have read their sublime lessons of wisdom and hope, and peace and warning, to the 'Sons of Light.' These same lessons, in the same language, they read to us to-day. But do we see in them what they did? Do they impress us as they did them? Or do they pass before our eyes like a panorama of some unknown land, which has no delineator to tell us what or where it is, or give us any intelligible notion regarding it? Accepting the symbol, have we lost its sense. Our Rites will be of little value to us if this is the case. It is our duty then, to make Freemasonry the object of a profound study. *We must consult the past.*

212. "We must stand by the sarcophagus of the murdered Osiris, in Egypt; enter the caverns of Phrygia, and hold communion with the Cabiti; penetrate the 'Collegia Fabrorum' of ancient Rome, and work in the Mystic Circles of Sidon. In a word, we must pursue our researches until we find the *thought* that lay in the minds of those who created the institu-

---

*Pierson, "Tradition or Masonry."

tion and founded our Mysteries. Then we shall know precisely what they mean. We shall see in them a grand series of moral and philosophical dramas, most eloquent and instructive, gleaming with sublime ideas, as the heavens glow with stars. And, finally, we shall discover that our Rites embrace all the possible circumstances of man—moral, spiritual, and social—and have a meaning high as heaven, broad as the universe, and profound as eternity."*

213. "If we seek the origin and first beginning of the Masonic philosophy, we must go away back into the ages of remote antiquity, when we shall find this beginning in the bosom of kindred associations, where the same philosophy was maintained and taught. But if we confound the ceremonies of Masonry with the philosophy of Masonry, and see the origin of the institution, moulded into outward form as it is to-day, we can scarcely be required to look farther back than the beginning of the eighteenth century, and, indeed, not quite so far.

214. "I contend that the philosophy of Freemasonry is engaged in the contemplation of the divine and human character; of God as one eternal, self-existent being, in contradiction to the mythology of the ancient peoples, which was burdened with a multitude of gods and goddesses, of demigods and heroes; of *man* as an immortal being, preparing in the present life for an eternal future, in like contradiction to the

---

*Sickels, "Ahiman Rezon."

ancient philosophy, which circumscribed the existence of man to the present life.''

215. ''These two doctrines, then, the unity of God and the immortality of the soul, constitute the philosophy of Freemasonry. When we wish to define it succinctly, we say that it is an ancient system of philosophy which teaches these two dogmas.''*

216. ''The fundamental law of Masonry requires only a belief in the Supreme Architect of the universe, and in a future life, while it says, with peculiar tolerance, that in all other matters of religious belief, Masons are only expected to be of that religion in which all men agree, leaving their particular opinions to themselves. Under the shelter of this wise provision, the Christian and the Jew, the Mohammedan and the Brahmin, are permitted to unite around our common altar, and Masonry becomes, in practice as well as in theory, universal. The truth is, that Masonry is undoubtedly a religious institution—its religion being of that universal kind in which all men agree, and which, handed down through a long succession of ages, from that ancient priesthood who first taught it, embraces the great tenets of the existence of God and the Immortality of the Soul— tenets which, by its peculiar symbolic language, it has preserved from its foundation, and still continues, in the same beautiful way, to teach. Beyond this, for its religious faith, we must not and cannot go.''* *

---

*Mackey, ''The Symbolism of Freemasonry.''
* *Mackey, ''Masonic Jurisprudence.''

217. "Freemasonry does not profess to interfere with the religious opinions of its members. It asks only for a declaration of that simple and universal faith, in which men of all nations and all sects agree— the belief in a God and in his superintending providence. Beyond this, it does not venture, but leaves the minds of its disciples, on other and sectarian points, perfectly untrammelled. This is the only religious qualification required by a candidate, but this is most strictly demanded. The religion, then, of Masonry, is pure theism, on which its different members engraft their own peculiar opinions; but they are not permitted to introduce them into the lodge, or to connect their truths or falsehood with the truth of Masonry."*

218. "Every Mason," says the old Charges of 1722, "is obliged by his tenure to obey the moral law." Now, this moral law is not to be considered as confined to the decalogue of Moses, within which narrow limits these ecclesiastical writers technically restrain it, but rather as alluding to what is called *Lex Naturae,* or the law of nature. This law of nature has been defined by an able, but not recent writer on this subject, to be "The will of God, relating to human actions, grounded on the moral differences of things; and because discoverable by natural light, obligatory upon all mankind."** This is the "Moral law," to which the old Charge already cited refers, and which it de-

---

*Mackey, "Masonic Lexicon."

* *Grove, "System of Moral Philosophy."

clares to be the law of Masonry. And this was wisely done, for it is evident that no law less universal could have been appropriately selected for the government of an institution whose prominent characteristic is its universality.

219. "The precepts of Jesus could not have been made obligatory on a Jew; a Christian would have denied the sanctions of the Koran; a Mohammedan must have rejected the laws of Moses; and a disciple of Zoroaster would have turned from all to the teachings of his Zeud Avesta. The universal law of nature, which the authors of the old Charges have properly called the moral law, because it is, as Conybeare remarks, 'a perfect collection of all those moral doctrines and precepts which have a foundation in the nature and reason of things,' is therefore the only law suited, in every respect, to be adopted as the Masonic code."*

220. "So broad is the religion of Masonry, and so carefully are all sectarian tenets excluded from the system, that the Christian, the Jew, and the Mohammedan, in all their numberless sects and divisions, may, and do harmoniously combine in its moral and intellectual work with the Buddhist, the Parsee, the Confucian, and the worshiper of Deity under every form."**

221. And why is this true? Because the Vishnu of the Brahminical Trinity, the Isis of the Egyptian and the Holy Ghost of the Christians and symbolized in

*Mackey, "Masonic Jurisprudence."
**Webb's "Monitor of Freemasonry."

the Roman Catholic Church, by the Madonna, is the Mother Principle of *every living thing in* the universe, and, when a man or woman has their spiritual mind awakened they have a love for everything that lives and breathes, and they look on every object in Nature as the outward manifestation of the Divine Living Principle *within*. God is in all, and no matter at what Shrine we worship, God is there.

222. "The whole design of Freemasonry as a Speculative science is the investigation of Divine Truths. To this great object everything else is subsidiary. The Mason is, from the time of his initiation as an Entered Apprentice, to the time at which he receives the full fruition of Masonic light, an investigator—a laborer in the quarry and the temple—whose reward is to be *truth*, and all the ceremonies and traditions of the order tend to this ultimate design. In Speculative Freemasonry there is an advancement from a lower to a higher state—from darkness to light—from death to life—from error to *truth*.

223. "The Mason living and working in the world as his lodge, must seek to raise himself out of it to that eminence which surmounts it, where alone he can find *divine truth*."*

224. "Every Speculative Mason is familiar with the fact that the East, as the source of material light, is a *symbol* of his *own* order, which professes to contain *within* its bosom the pure light of truth. As, in

*Mackey, "Manual of the Lodge."

the physical world, the morning of each day is ushered into existence by the reddening dawn of the Eastern sky, whence the rising sun dispenses his illuminating and prolific rays to every portion of the visible horizon, warming the whole earth with his embrace of light, and giving new-born life and energy to flowers and tree, and beast and man, who, at the magic touch, awake from the sleep of darkness, so *in the moral world, when intellectual night was, in the earliest days, brooding over the world, it was from the Ancient Priesthood living in the East that those lessons of God, of Nature, and of Humanity first emanated, which, traveling Westward, revealed to man his future destiny, and his dependence on a Superior Power. Thus every new and true doctrine, coming from these 'Wise Men of the East,' was, as it were, a new day rising, and dissipating the clouds of intellectual darkness and error. It was a universal opinion among the Ancients that the first learning came from the East (and a very true one); and the often-quoted line of Bishop Berkeley, that—*
'Westward the course of empire takes its way'— *is but the modern utterance of an Ancient thought, for it was always believed that the empire of Truth and Knowledge was advancing from the East to the West.''*

226. Mystic Masonry, which naturally includes Craft Masonry, holds within itself the only true religion now in the world, that Divine Truth which

*Mackey, "Symbolism of Freemasonry."

guides man in his pilgrimage through life, and confers on its initiates such knowledge and science that nothing more is required by the Soul in its onward Path. It is not only the repository of Religion, but it holds the Key to *all* Religion.

227. "Freemasonry itself anciently received, among other appellations, that of Lux, or Light, to signify that it is to be regarded as that Sublime doctrine of Divine Truth by which the path of him who has attained it is to be illuminated in his pilgrimage through life.

228. "Light was, in accordance with the old religious sentiment, the great object of attainment in all the Ancient religious Mysteries. It was there, as it is now, in Masonry, made the symbol of *truth* and *knowledge*. This was always its ancient symbolism, and we must never lose sight of this emblematic meaning, when we are considering the nature and significance of Masonic light.

229. "In all the ancient systems this reverence for light, as the symbol of truth, was predominant. In the Mysteries of every nation, the candidate was made to pass, during his initiation, through scenes of utter darkness, and at length terminated his trials by an admission to the splendidly-illuminated sacellum, or sanctuary, where he was said to have attained pure and perfect light, and where he received the necessary instructions which were to invest him with that knowledge of the Divine Truth which it had been the object of all his labors to gain, and the design of the

institution, into which he had been initiated, to bestow.

230. "Light, therefore, became synonymous with *truth* and *knowledge*, and *darkness* with *falsehood* and *ignorance*. We find this symbolism pervading not only the institutions, but the very languages, of antiquity."*

231. "It is a Landmark, that a "Book of the Law' shall constitute an indispensable part of the furniture of every Lodge. I say advisedly, a *Book of the Law*, because it is not absolutely required that everywhere the Old and New Testament shall be used. The 'Book of the Law' is that volume which, by the religion of the country, is believed to contain the revealed will of the Great Architect of the Universe. Hence, in all Lodges in Christian countries, the Book of the Law is composed of the Old and New Testaments; in a country where Judaism was the prevailing faith, the Old Testament alone would be sufficient; and in Mohammedan countries, and among Mohammedan Masons the Koran might be substituted. Masonry does not attempt to interfere with the peculiar religious faith of its disciples, except so far as relates to the belief in the existence of God, and what necessarily results from that belief. The Book of Law is to the speculative Mason his spiritual Trestle-board; without this he cannot labour; whatever he believes to be the revealed will of the Grand Architect constitutes for him his Spiritual Trestle-

*Mackey, "Symbolism of Freemasonry."

board; and must ever be before him in his hours of speculative labor, to be the rule and guide of his conduct. The Landmark, therefore, requires that a Book of the Law, a religious code of some kind, purporting to be an examplar of the revealed will of God, shall form an essential part of the furniture of every Lodge.''*

·· 232. The Holy Bible of the Christian is no better to *the* Christian than is the Koran to the Mohammedan. Each believes that *his* faith is the only *true* one and so long as each one does as he truly believes and lets his brother do the same, they are both right. How can the Christian say that *his* alone is the true religion? Such a thing is foolish and bigoted and there is no Christianity in it. The Oath of the Mohammedan would be of no value if taken on the Holy Bible, *because he does not believe in the Bible.* Mystic Masonry respects the religion of each and every one, *knowing that the foundation of each sect is the same as that of the other.*

233. The religious philosophy of Masonry is as old as is the First religion, for Masonry itself is founded on the Mysteries of Antiquity, which was already taught on the lost Atlantis.

234. "Egypt was repeopled after the deluge by the sons of Ham, and they made more rapid advances in recovering a knowledge of the arts and science, partially lost by that catastrophe, than any other people, until Egypt became to be looked upon as the mother

*Mackey, "Masonic Jurisprudence."

of science. Philosophers of all nations resorted there for instructions and initiation, and writers generally assert that her religious system was borrowed by all other nations. Hence it is said the reason why Saturn, Jupiter, Neputine, Bacchus, Gionysius, Adonis, Hu, Schiva, Brahma, Odin, Fohi, etc., were said but to be other names for Osiris; and Venus, Astrate, Juno, Ceres, Proserpine, Cerdeiven, Frea, Rhea, Sita, etc., of Isis. *The legends of every one of the different phases of the mysteries, irrespective of country or language, had the same general character; in fact, were all identical except in the name of individuals.* Each legend represented the death, by violence, of some particular person; with some it was a god, with others a demi-god, and with others a great warrior or person who had conferred signal benefits upon man in agricultural pursuits, or in the arts and sciences. In consequence of such death something was lost; there was then a search made for that which was lost, a finding of it, or of a part of it, or of something that was adopted as a substitute for it—a beginning in sorrow and lamentation, and an ending in joy and rejoicing. Such is a brief summary of the legend that accompanied the ceremonial of each of the systems of the mysteries of which we have an account, either historical or traditional, that has been practiced on this globe. We have presented that of the Egyptian Mysteries because it has been generally regarded as the parent *of all others*. More pages of the writings of the ancients that have been preserved to our times are devoted to the mysteries than to the development of empires. Hence we have a better knowledge of the ceremonial and legend of many of the phases of the mysteries than we have of the country in which they were practiced.

235. "That all the mysteries throughout the world were the same in substance, being derived from *one* source, and celebrated in honor of the same Deities, though acknowledged under different appellations, is further evidenced from the fact that they are traced to the plains of Shinar before the dispersion of mankind.

236. "They were introduced, so says tradition, into India by Brahma, into China and Japan by Buddha, into Egypt by Troth, the son of Mizraim (some say by Mizraim himself), into Persia by Zeradhust, into Greece by Melampus or Cadmus, into Boeotia by Promospus or Dardanus, into Messene by Caucon, into Thebes by Methapus, into Athens by Erectheus, into Etruria by Philostratus, into the city of Arene by Lycus, into Thrace by Orpheus, into Italy by the Pelasgi, into Cyprus by Cinyras, into Gaul and Britain by Gomer, or his immediate Descendants, into Scandinavia by Sigge or Odin, into Mexico by Vitzliputzli, and into Peru by Manco Capac and his wife—*and into Judea by Hiram Abif.*"*

237. "Egypt was the cradle of all the Mysteries. At one time in possession of all the learning and religion that was to be found in the world, it extended into other nations the influence of its sacred rites and

*Pierson, "Traditions of Freemasonry."

its Secret Doctrines. The importance, therefore, of the Egyptian Mysteries will entitle them to a more diffusive explanation than has been awarded to the examination of the other rites.

238. "The priesthood of Egypt constituted a sacred caste, in whom the sacerdotal functions were hereditary. They exercised also an important part in the government of the state, and the kings of Egypt were but the first subjects of the priests. They had originally organized, and continued to control the ceremonies of initiation. Their doctrines were of two kinds, the Exoteric or public, which were communicated to the multitude, and Esoteric or secret, which were revealed only to a chosen few; and to obtain them it was necessary to pass through an initiation, which, as we shall see, was characterized by the severest trials of courage and fortitude.

239. "The principal seat of the Mysteries was at Memphis, in the neighborhood of the great Pyramid (*within* the Pyramid). They were of two kinds, the greater and the less; the former being the mysteries of Osiris and Serapis; the latter those of Isis."*

240. "Mysteries was the name given to those religious assemblies of the ancients, whose ceremonies were conducted in secret, whose doctrines were known only to those who had obtained the right of knowledge by a previous initiation, and whose members were in possession of signs and tokens by which they were enabled to recognize each other. For the origin of

*Mackey, "Lexicon of Freemasonry."

these Mysteries we must look to the Gymnosophists of India, from whom they passed through Egypt into Greece and Rome, and from whom likewise they were extended, in a more immediate line, to the northern part of Europe and to Britain. The most important of the mysteries were those of Mithras, celebrated in Persia; or Osiris and Isis, celebrated in Egypt; of Eleusis, instituted in Greece; and the Scandinavian and Druidical rites, which were confined to the Gothic and Celtic tribes. In all these various mysteries, we find a singular unity of design clearly indicating a common origin, and a purity of doctrine as evidently proving that this common origin was not to be sought for in the popular theology of the Pagan world. The ceremonies of initiation were all funereal in their character. They celebrated the death and the resurrection of some cherished being, either the object of esteem as a hero, or of devotion as a god. Subordination of degrees was instituted, and the candidate was subjected to probations varying in their character and severity; the rites were practiced in the darkness of night, and often amid the gloom of impenetrable forests or subterranean caverns; and the full fruition of knowledge, for which so much labor was endured, and so much danger incurred, was not attained until the aspirant, well tried and thoroughly purified, had reached the place of wisdom and light."*

241. Among all the Ancient people there was both a Public and a Secret worship. The Secret worship

---

*Mackey, "Lexicon of Freemasonry."

did not originate in Egypt, but in Ancient Atlantis and from thence to Egypt. The Secret Worship has always been known as "The Mysteries" and there is no doubt but that these Mysteries were the same in Substance, in the religious philosophy, *their legends and the very foundation was the same.* These Mysteries could only be obtained by Initiation, and the members of such Orders were always known by signs or tokens. This Secret Worship or Initiation was *not* because the Initiates did *not want the people to know the secrets, but because the people were not able to receive the knowledge.* It is foolish to say that the Priests of the Mysteries wanted to keep the people in ignorance. *Such was not the case,* but the masses have never been able to receive these mysteries nor can they at the present time.

242. "The qualification for initiation (in the Mysteries of Greece) were maturity of age, and purity of conduct. A character, free from suspicion of immorality, was absolutely required in the aspirant. Nero, on this account, did not dare, when in Greece, to offer himself as a candidate for initiation. The privilege was at first confined to natives of Greece, but it was afterwards extended to foreigners. Significant symbols were used as means of instructions, and words of recognition were communicated to the initiated.

243. "In these regulations, as well as in the gradual advancement of the candidate from one degree to another, that resemblance to our own institution is

readily perceived, which has given these, as well as to other ancient mysteries, the appropriate name of Spurious Freemasonry."*

244. "These Mysteries existed in every country of heathendom, in each under a different name, and to some extent under a different form, but always and everywhere with the same design of inculcating, by allegorical and symbolic teachings, the great Masonic doctrine of the Unity of God and the Immortality of the Soul. . This is an important proposition, and the fact which it enunciates must never be lost sight of in an inquiry into the origin of Freemasonry; for the pagan Mysteries were to the spurious Freemasonry of antiquity precisely what the Masters' lodge are to the Freemasonry of the present day. It is needless to offer any proof of their existence, since this is admitted and continually referred to by all historians, ancient and modern; and to discuss minutely their character and organization would occupy a distinct treatise."**

245. "The legend and traditions of 'Hiram *Abif* (for such is the rendering of the Hebrew text in Luther's Bible)' form the consummation of the connecting links between Freemasonry and the Ancient Mysteries, and sustains beyond peradventure the theory that Freemasonry dates anterior to the Deluge and the strong probability of its divine origin.

246. "We do not assert that the legend of Hiram

---

*Mackey, "Lexicon of Freemasonry."
**Mackey, "Symbolism of Freemasonry."

9a

Abif is true. We only know that it has come to us by
tradition. At what time the legend of the death of
Hiram Abif took the place of the older legends in the
Mysteries of Persia, India, Egypt, etc., we have no
information. Nor is it important for us to know; for
Masonry is a succession of allegories, the mere vehicles
of great lessons in morality and Philosophy.

247. ''The Masonic legend stands by itself, unsup-
ported by history or other than its own traditions; yet
we readily recognize in Hiram Abif, one of the Grand
Masters of Freemasons, the Osiris of the Egyptians,
the Mithras of the Persians, the Bacchus of the
Greeks, the Dionysius of the Fraternity of the Artificers, and the Atys of the Phrygians, whose passion,
death and resurrection were celebrated by these people
respectively.

248. ''For many ages and everywhere Masons have
celebrated the death of Hiram Abif. That event,
therefore, interests the whole world and no particular
sect, order or coterie; it belongs to no particular time,
religion or people. Everywhere among the ancient
nations there existed a similar allegory, and all must
refer to the same great primitive fact. *That fact we
believe to have been the murder of Abel by his brother
Cain.*

249. ''In the Apprentice we find reproduced the
Aspirant of Thebes and Eleusis, the Soldiers of Mithras, the Christian Catechumen. In the Fellow Craft,
the........of Eleusis the Initiate of the Second
Order, the Lion of the Eastern Mysteries, the Chris-

tian Neophyte. In all the Mysteries there was a double doctrine. It was so everywhere. The Brahmins of India as well as among the Druids of Germany and Gaul, at Memphis, Samothrace and Eleusis; in the Mysteries of the Hebrews and early Christians as well as in those of Ceres and the Good Goddess. Everywhere we see emblems presenting a physical meaning and receiving a double interpretation; one natural and, as it were, material, within the reach of ordinary intellects; the other, sublime and philosophical, which was communicated to those men of genius only who, in the preparatory degree, had understood the concealed meaning of the allegories.

250. "Everywhere in the East (*and Christ was in the East*), the cradle of religions and allegories, we see in ancient times under different names the same idea reproduced; everywhere a god, a supreme being or an extraordinary man is slain to recommence afterwards a glorious life; everywhere we meet the memory of a great tragical event, a crime or transgression that plunges the people into sorrow and mourning, to which soon succeeds enthusiastic rejoicing."*

251. "The *Mysteries of Osiris* formed the third degree or summit of the Egyptian Initiation. In these, the legend of the murder of Osiris, by his brother Typhon, was represented, and the god was personated by the candidate. Osiris, according to the tradition, was a wise king of Egypt, who having

---

*Piersons, "Traditions of Freemasonry."

achieved the reform of his subjects at home, resolved
to spread the blessings of civilization in the other
parts of the earth. This he accomplished, but on his
return he found his kingdom, which he had left in the
care of his wife Isis, distracted by the seditions of his
brother Typhon.   Osiris attempted, by mild re-
monstrances, to convince his brother of the impro-
priety of his conduct, but he fell a sacrifice in the
attempt.   For Typhon murdered him in a secret
apartment, and cutting up the body, enclosed the
pieces in a chest, which he committed to the waters of
the Nile.   Isis, searching for the body, found it, and
entrusted it to the care of the priests, establishing at
the same time the Mysteries in commemoration of the
foul deed.   One piece of the body, however, she could
not find, the *Membrum Virile*. For this she substituted a fictitious representation, which she consecrated, and which, under the name of *Phallus*, is to
be found as the emblem of fecundity in *all* the Ancient
Mysteries.

252. "This legend was purely astronomical. Osiris
was the sun, Isis the moon. Typhon was the symbol
of winter, which destroys the fecundating and fer-
tilizing powers of the sun, thus, as it were, depriving
him of life. This was the catastrophe celebrated in
the Mysteries, and the aspirant was made to pass
fictitiously through the sufferings and the death of
Osiris."*

253. "The idea of the existence of an enlightened

*Mackey, "Lexicon of Freemasonry."

people who lived at a remote era, and came from the east, was a very prevalent notion among the Ancient traditions. Ezekiel in verse 2, chapter xliii, says: 'The glory of the God of Israel came from the way of the East.' Adam Clark says: 'All knowledge, all religion, and all arts and science have traveled according to the course of the sun from east to west.' Bazot tells us in his *Manuel du Franc-Macon*, page 154, that 'the veneration which Masons entertain for the east confirms an opinion previously announced, that the religious system of Masonry came from the east, and has reference to the *Primitive Religion*, whose first occupation was the worship of the sun.'*

254. "Among the Egyptians, too, the chief deity, Osiris, was but another name for the sun, while his arch-enemy and destroyer, Typhon, was the typification of the night, or darkness. And lastly, among the Hindu, the three manifestations of their supreme Deity, Brahma, Siva, and Vishni, were symbols of the rising meridian, and setting Sun."

255. "This early and very general prevalence of the sentiment of sun-worship is worthy of especial attention on account of the influence that it exercised over the spurious Freemasonry of antiquity,........ Many, indeed, nearly all, of the Masonic symbols of the present day can only be thoroughly understood and properly appreciated by this reference to sun-worship.

---

*Piersan, "Tradition of Freemasonry."

256. "One thing, at least, is incapable of refutation, and that is, that we are indebted to the Tyrian Masons for the introduction of the symbol of Hiram Abif. The idea of the symbol, although modified .by the Jewish Masons, is *not* Jewish in its inception. It was evidently borrowed from the pagan Mysteries, where Bacchus, Adonis, Proserpine, and a host of other apotheosized beings play the same role that Hiram does in the Masonic Mysteries."*

257. "In every country under heaven the initiations were performed in caverns, either natural or artificial, and *darkness* was honored with peculiar marks of veneration, by reason of its supposed priority of existence. 'And God said, Let there be light: and there was Light.' Light was an emblem of Life, and Darkness of death; and Death was a prelude to resurrection. It will at once be seen, therefore, in what manner the doctrine of the resurrection was inculcated and exemplified in these remarkable institutions of the ancients."**

258. "In all the ancient systems of Initiation the candidate was shrouded in darkness, as a preparation for the reception of light. The duration varied in the different rites. In the Celtic Mysteries of Druidism, the period in which the aspirant was immersed in darkness was nine days and nights; among the Greeks, at Eleusis, it was three times as long; and in the still severer rites of Mithras, in Persia, fifty

---

*Mackey, "Symbolism of Freemasonry."
**Pierson, "Traditions of Freemasonry."

days of darkness, solitude and fasting were imposed upon the adventurous neophyte, who by these excessive trials, was at length entitled to the full communication of the light of knowledge.

259. "Darkness, like death, is the symbol of Initiation. It was for this reason that all the ancient initiations were performed at night. The same custom prevails in Freemasonry, and the explanation is the same. Death and the Resurrection were taught in the Mysteries, as they are in Freemasonry. The initiation was the lesson of death. The full fruition or autopsy, the reception of light, was the lesson of Regeneration or Resurrection."

260. "Light is, therefore, a fundamental symbol in Freemasonry. It is, in fact, the first important symbol that is presented to the neophyte in his instructions, and contains within itself the very essence of Speculative Masonry, which is nothing more than the contemplation of intellectual light or truth."*

261. "A laudable thirst after knowledge prompted the youth of all ranks to aspire to the ambition of deciphering the meaning and illustration of those obscure symbols, which were said to have been communicated to the priests by the revelation from the celestial Deities. Initiation was the only means of acquiring this knowledge, and it is therefore no wonder that initiation was so much in request.

262. "There was also another quality of the mind which served to recommend the mysteries:—that

*Mackey, "Symbolism of Freemasonry."

strange attachment to the marvelous by which every grade of human nature is swayed. To excite this sentiment in all its sublimity of horror, the initiations were performed at the dead of night. No severity of probation could deter the bold and determined aspirant from encountering terrors and actual dangers which led to the gratification of his curiosity; and the shades of darkness imparted vigor to the passion which looked forward to a recompense of such an exalted nature."*

263. "In the Old Lectures it is said, 'He that is truly square, well polished, and uprightly fixed, is qualified to be a member of our most honorable society. He that trusteth such a person with any engagement is freed from all trouble and anxiety about the performance of it, for he is faithful to his trust; his words are the breathings of his heart, and he is an utter stranger to deceit.'

264. "In the Mysteries of India, the aspirant was invested with a consecrated sash or girdle, which he was directed to wear next his skin. It was manufactured with many mysterious ceremonies, and said to possess the power of preserving the wearer from *personal danger*. It consisted of a cord composed of *three times three* threads twisted together and fastened at the end with a knot, and was called *Zennar*. Hence comes our Cable-tow. It was an emblem of their triune Deity, the remembrance of

*Oliver, "History of Initiation."

whom we also preserve in many of our symbols.''*

265. ''The *rite of discalceation,* or uncovering the feet on approaching holy ground, is derived from the Latin word *discalceare,* to pluck off one's shoes. The usage has the prestige of antiquity and universality in its favor.

266. ''That it not only very generally prevailed, but that its symbolic signification was well understood in the days of Moses, we learn from that passage of Exodus where the angel of the Lord, at the burning bush, exclaims to the patriarch, 'Draw not nigh hither; put off thy shoes from off thy feet, for the place whereon thou standest is holy ground.' Clark thinks it is from this command that the Eastern nations have derived the custom of performing all their acts of religious worship with bare feet. But it is much more probable that the ceremony was in use long anterior to the circumstances of the burning bush, and that the Jewish lawgiver at once recognized it as a well-known sign of reverence.

267. ''Bishop Patrick entertains this opinion, and thinks that the custom was derived from the ancient patriarchs, and was transmitted by a general tradition to succeeding times.

268. ''The direction of Pythagoras to his disciples was in these words: 'Offer sacrifices and worship with thy shoes off.'

269. ''The Mohammedans, when about to perform

*Pierson, ''Traditions of Freemasonry.''

their devotions, always leave their slippers at the
door of the mosque. The Druids practiced the same
custom whenever they celebrated their sacred rites;
and the ancient Peruvians are said always to have
left their shoes at the porch when they entered the
magnificent temple consecrated to the worship of the
sun.

270. "Adam Clark thinks that the custom of wor-
shipping the Deity barefooted was so general among
all nations of antiquity, that he assigns it as one of his
thirteen proofs *that the whole human race have been
derived from one family.*

271. "The rite of discalceation is, therefore, a
symbol of reverence. It signifies, in the language of
symbolism, that the spot which is about to be ap-
proached in this humble and reverential manner is
consecrated to some holy purpose.

272. "Into the Master Mason's lodge—this holy of
holies of the Masonic temple, where the solemn truths
of death and immortality are inculcated—the
aspirant, on entering, should purify his heart from
every contamination, and remember, with a due sense
of their symbolic application, those words that once
l·roke upon the astonished ears of the old patriarch,
'Put off thy shoes from off thy feet, for the place
whereon thou standest is holy ground.' ''*

273. "In the ancient initiation the candidate was
never permitted to enter on the threshold of the

---

*Mackey, "Symbolism of Freemasonry."

temple, or sacred cavern in which the ceremonies were to be conducted, until, by the most solemn warning, he had been impressed with the necessity of caution, secrecy and fortitude."*

274. "The probation of a candidate in ancient times embraced many important particulars; but principally his fortitude and constancy were severely tried by the application of—sometimes an iron instrument heated red hot; at others the point of a sword or other sharp weapon, while he himself was deprived of all means of defense and protection.

275. "Freemasonry is a system based upon the knowledge and acknowledgement of God, who is the creator of the world and the author and giver of every good and perfect gift; the vehicle which has brought down from the antediluvian world the primitive religion of man. It must not, however, be mistaken for a religious *sect*, although it embraces that universal system in which all men agree, while the infidel and atheist are *excluded* because they prefer the dangerous alternative of disbelieving the Divine existence."* *

276. "The successful probationer, at the expiration of his novitiate, was brought forth into the cavern of initiation, where he entered on the point of a sword presented to his naked left breast, by which he was slightly wounded, and then he was ritually prepared for the approaching ceremony. He was crowned with olive, anointed with oil of *ban*, and armed with en-

---

*Mackey, "Manual of the Lodge."
* *Pierson, "Traditions of Freemasonry."

chanted armour, by his guide, who was the representative of simorgh, a monstrous griffin, and an important agent in the machinery of Persian mythology, and furnished with talismans that he might be ready to encounter all the hideous monsters raised up by the Dives to impede his progress to perfection. Induced into an inner apartment he was purified with fire*
and water, and solemnly put through the Seven Stages of initiation. From the precipice where he stood, he beheld a deep and dangerous vault into which a single false step might precipitate him down to the 'Throne of dreadful necessity,' which was an emblem of those infernal regions through which he was about to pass. Threading the circuitous mazes of the gloomy cavern, he was soon awakened from his trance of thought, by seeing the sacred fire, at intervals, flash through its recesses to illuminate his path; sometimes bursting from beneath his feet; sometimes descending on his head in a broad sheet of white and shadowy flame. Amidst the admiration thus inspired, his terror was excited by the distant yelling of ravenous beasts; the roaring of lions, the howling of wolves, the fierce and threatening bark of dogs, etc."**

277. "The *circumambulation* among the pagan nations referred to the great doctrine of Sabaism, or Sun-worship. Freemasonry alone has preserved the primitive meaning, which was a symbolic allusion to the sun, as the source of physical light and the most

---

*See "The Philosophy of Fire."
* *Oliver, "History of Initiation."

wonderful work of the Grand Architect of the Universe. The lodge represents the world; the three principal officers represent the sun in her three principal positions—at rising, at meridian, and at setting. The *circumambulation*, therefore, alludes to the apparent course of the solar orb, through these points around the world."*

278. "In the rite of circumambulation we find another ceremony borrowed from the Ancient Freemasonry that was practiced in the Mysteries. In Ancient Greece, when the priests were engaged in the rite of sacrifice, they and the people always walked *three times* round the altar while singing a sacred hymn. In making this procession great care was taken to move in imitation of the course of the sun. For this purpose they commenced at the east, and passing on by the way of the south to the west, and thence by the north, they arrived at the east again. By this means, as it will be observed, the right hand was always nearest the altar.

279. "Among the Romans the ceremony of circumambulation was always used in the rites of sacrifice, of expiation, of purification. Thus Virgil describes Corynoeus as purifying his companions at the funeral of Misenus, by passing *three* times around them while aspersing them with the lustral waters, and to do so conveniently it was necessary that he should have moved with his right hand toward them.

---

*Mackey, "Manual of the Lodge."

10

280. "Among the Hindus the same rite of circum-ambulation has always been practiced. As an instance, we may cite the ceremonies which are required to be performed by a Brahmin upon first rising from bed in the morning. The priest having first adored the sun, while directing his face to the east, then walks toward the west by the way of the south, saying at the same time, 'I follow the course of the sun,' which he thus explains: 'As the sun in his course moves round the world by the way of the south, so do I follow that luminary, to obtain the benefit arising from a journey round the earth by the way of the south.' "*

281. "Among the Ancients Silence and Secrecy were considered virtues of the highest order. The Egyptians worshipped Harpocrates, the god of secrecy, raised altars in his name, and wreathed them with garlands of flowers. Among the Ancient Romans these virtues were not less esteemed, and a distinguished Latin poet tells us, 'for faithful silence also there is a sure reward.' "* *

282. "An oath taken with the face toward the east was deemed more solemn and binding than when taken with the face toward any other cardinal point. Oaths were variously confirmed by lifting up the hands to heaven, by placing them on the altar, or on a stone, or in the hands of the person administering the oath; and a most solemn method of confirming an

---

*Pierson, "Tradition of Freemasonry."
**Sickles, "Freemason's Guide."

oath was by *placing a drawn sword across the throat* of the person to whom it was administered, and invoking heaven, earth and sea to witness the ratification.

283. "It was the custom to add a solemn imprecation to their oaths, either for the satisfaction of the person by whom the oath was imposed, or to lay a more inviolable obligation on themselves, lest they should at any time repent of their purpose and take contrary measures to what they then resolved upon. The person who took the oath in some of the mysterious rites was to be upon his bare knees, with a naked sword pointed to his throat."*

284. "The right hand has in all ages been deemed an emblem of fidelity and the Ancients worshipped Deity under the name *Fides*, or Fidelity, which was sometimes represented by two right hands joined and sometimes by two human figures holding each other by the right hand."* *

285. "Valerius Maximus tells us that the Ancients had a moral Deity whom they called Fides. Her temple was first consecrated by Numa. Fides was a Goddess of honesty and fidelity; and the writer adds, when they promised anything of old they gave the right hand to pledge it, as we do, and therefore she is represented as giving her hand and sometimes her two hands conjoining. Chartarius more fully describes this by observing that the proper residence of

*Pierson, "Traditions of Freemasonry."
* *Sickles, "General Ahiman Rezon."

faith or fidelity was thought by the Ancients to be in the right hand. And therefore this Deity was sometimes represented by two right hands joined together; sometimes by two little images shaking each other's right hand, so that the right hand was by them held sacred, and was symbolically made use of in a solemn manner to denote fidelity.

286. "In the Scriptures we find frequent references to the use of the right hand, either in confirmation of an agreement or as an emblem of truth and fidelity. Thus St. Paul says: 'When James, Cephas, and John, who seemed to be pillars, perceived the grace that was given unto me, they gave me and Barnabas the *right hands* of fellowship, that *we* should go unto the *heathen,* and *they* unto the *circumcision.*' In Psalms it is said, 'Their right hand is a right hand of falsehood,' that is to say, they lift up their right hand to swear to what is not true.

287. "This lifting up the right hand was, in fact, the universal mode adopted among both Jews and Pagans (and is still at the present time) in taking an oath. The custom is certainly older than the days of Abram, who said to the king of Sodom, 'I have lift up mine hand unto the Lord, the most high God, the possessor of heaven and earth, that I will not take anything that is thine.' The mode of expression shows that the uplifting of the right hand was a familiar emblem, and recognized as an evidence of truth.'"*

---

*Pierson, "Traditions of Freemasonry."

288. "The Rite of Illumination is a very Ancient ceremony, and constitutes an important feature in all the mysteries of the early ages. In the Egyptian, Cabirian, Sidonian, Eleusinian, Scandinavian and Druidical rituals it held a prominent place, and in them all represented the same ideas. It marked the termination of the Mystic pilgrimage through gloom and night, and was emblematical of the moral and intellectual light, which pours its Divine radiance on the mind after it has conquered the prejudice, and passions, and ignorance,* with which it has so long been struggling."**

289. "Light was, in accordance with the old religious sentiment, the great object of attainment in all the Ancient Religious Mysteries. It was there, as it is now, in Masonry, made the symbol of *truth* and *knowledge.* This was always its ancient symbolism, and we must never lose sight of this emblematic meaning, when we are considering the nature and signification of Masonic light. When the candidate makes a demand for light, it is not merely for that material light which is to remove a physical darkness; that is only the outward form, which conceals the *inward* symbolism. He craves an intellectual illumination which will dispel the darkness of mental and moral ignorance, and bring to his view, as an eyewitness, the Sublime Truths of Religion, Phil-

---

*See "The Philosophy of Fire," Chapter on the Initiation of *the* Christ.

**Sickles, "Freemason's Guide."

osophy, and Science, which it is the great design of
(*true*) Freemasonry to teach.

290. "In all the Ancient systems this reverence for
light, as the symbol of truth, was predominant. In
the Mysteries of every nation, the candidate was made
to pass, during his initiations, through scenes of utter
darkness, and at length terminated his trials by an
admission to the splendidly-illuminated sacellum, or
sanctuary, where he was said to have attained pure
and perfect light, and where he received the necessary
instructions which were to invest him with that
knowledge of the Divine Truth which it had been the
object of all his labors to gain, and the design of the
institution, into which he had been initiated, to bestow."*

291. "The Rite of Intrusting supplies us with many
important and interesting symbols. There is an important period in the ceremony of Masonic initiation,
where the candidate is about to receive a full communication of the Mysteries through which he has
passed, and to which the trials and labors which he
has undergone can only entitle him. This ceremony
is technically called the 'Rite of Intrusting,' because
it is then that the aspirant begins to be intrusted with
that for the possession of which he was seeking. It
is equivalent to what, in the Ancient Mysteries, was
called the 'autopsy,' or the seeing of what only the
initiated were permitted to see.

*Mackey, "Symbolism of Freemasonry."

292. "This Rite of Intrusting is, of course, divided into several parts or periods; for the *aporreta*, or secret things of Masonry, are not to be given at once, but in gradual progression. It begins, however, with the communication of Light, which, although but a preparation for the development of the mysteries which are to follow, must be considered as one of the most important symbols in the whole science of Masonic symbolism. So important, indeed, is it, and so much does it pervade with its influence and its relations the whole Masonic system, that Freemasonry itself anciently received, among other appellations, that of Lux, or Light, to signify that it is to be regarded as the Sublime Doctrine of Divine Truth by which the path of him who has attained it is to be illuminated in his pilgrimage of life."*

293. "Turning from the scenes of woe, he (the candidate) was passed through some other dark caverns and passages, until, having successfully treaded the labyrinth, consisting of six spacious vaults, connected by winding galleries, each opening with a narrow portal, the scene of some perilous adventure; and having, by the exercise of fortitude and perseverance, been triumphantly borne through this accumulated mass of difficulty and danger, the doors of the seventh vault, or Sacellum, were thrown open, and his darkness was changed into light. He was admitted into the spacious and lofty cavern already described, which was denominated the sacred grotto

*Mackey, "Symbolism of Freemasonry."

of Elysium. This consecrated place was brilliantly illuminated, and sparkled with gold and precious stones. A splendid sun, and starry system emitted their dazzling radiance, and moved in order to the symphonies of heavenly music. Here sat the Archimagus in the East, elevated on a throne of burnished gold, crowned with a rich diadem decorated with myrtle boughs, and habited in a flowing tunic of a bright cerulean tincture; round him were arranged in solemn order the Presules, and dispensers of the Mysteries; forming altogether a reverend assembly, which covered the awe-struck aspirant with a profound feeling of veneration; and, an involuntary impulse, frequently produced an act of worship. Here he was received with congratulations; and after having entered into the usual engagement for keeping secret the sacred Rite of Mithras, the Sacred Words were intrusted to him, of which the ineffable Tetractys, or name of God was the chief.''*

294. ''The Rite of Investiture, called, in the colloqually technical language of the order, the Ceremony of Clothing, brings us at once to the consideration of that well-known symbol of Freemasonry, the *Lambskin Apron*.

295. ''This Rite of Investiture, or the placing upon the aspirant some garment, as an indication of his appropriate preparation for the ceremonies in which he was about to engage, prevailed in all the Ancient institutions.

*Oliver, ''History of Initiation.''

, 296. "In the Levitical economy of the Israelites the priests always wore the abnet, or linen apron, or girdle, as a part of the investiture of the priesthood. This, with the other garments, was to be worn, as the text expresses it, 'for glory and for beauty,' or, as it has been explained by a learned commentator, 'as emblematical of that holiness and purity which ever characterize the Divine nature, and the worship which is worthy of Him.'

297. "In the Persian Mysteries of Mithras, the candidate, having first received light, was invested with a girdle, a crown of mitre, a purple tunic, and, lastly, a white apron.

298. "In the initiations practiced in Hindustan, in the ceremony of investiture was substituted the sash, or sacred zennaar, consisting of a cord, composed of nine threads twisted into a knot at the end, and hanging from the left shoulder to the right hip. This was, perhaps, the type of the Masonic scarf, which is, or ought to be, always worn in the same position.

299. "In the Scandinavian Rites, where the military genius of the people had introduced a warlike species of initiation, instead of the apron, we find the candidate receiving a white shield, which was, however, always presented with the accompaniment of some symbolic instructions, not very dissimilar to that which is connected with the Masonic apron.

300. "In the Apocalypse a *white stone* was the reward promised by the Spirit to those who overcame;

and in the same mystical book the apostle is instructed to say, that fine linen, clean and *white*, is the righteousness of the saints.

301. "In the early ages of the *(true)* Christian Church a *white garment* was *always* placed upon the catechumen who had been recently baptized, to denote that he had been cleansed from his former sins, and was thenceforth to lead a life of innocence and purity. Hence it was presented to him with this appropriate charge: 'Receive the white and undefiled garment, and produce it unspotted before the tribunal of our Lord Jesus Christ, that you may obtain Immortal life.' "*

301. "There is no one symbol of Masonry more important in its teachings, or more interesting in its history, than that of the lambskin or white leather apron. It is impressed upon the Mason's memory as the first gift which he receives, the first symbol that is explained to him, and the first tangible evidence which he possesses of his admission into the Fraternity.

302. "The apron or girdle, in ancient times, was a universally received emblem of truth and passive duty. The Israelites, when preparing to effect their escape from Egyptian captivity, were enjoined to eat the Passover with *their loins girded.*

303. "It was the firm opinion of the Essenes that internal purity and rectitude of conduct were strikingly evinced by a person's outward appearance.

---

* Mackey, "Symbolism of Freemasonry."

The belief was probably derived from that famous precept of King Solomon, who had constantly the same emblematical reference on his lips: *'Let thy garments be always white.'*

304. "When a candidate was initiated into the ancient mysteries, he was esteemed *regenerate;* and he was invested with a white garment and apron as a symbol of his newly attained purity.

305. "Among the Greeks the garment of initiation was white, because, says Cicero, 'white is the color most acceptable to the gods.' This robe was accounted sacred, and a never-failing source of protection in every emergency.

306. "All the ancient statues of the heathen gods which have been discovered in Egypt, Greece, Persia, Hindustan or America, are uniformly decorated with aprons. Hence is deducted the antiquity of this article of apparel."*

307. "The emblematical foundations or supports of a Masonic Lodge are three pillars, denominated Wisdom, Strength and Beauty. These three noble pillars give it a stability which no exertion of art or ingenuity can subvert, and no force can overthrow. They were thus named in allusion to the perfection with which our system has been endowed by the Almighty Architect: because, without wisdom to contrive, strength to support, and beauty to adore, no structure can be perfect.

---

*Pierson, "Traditions of Freemasonry."

308. "In the Ancient Mysteries these three pillars represented the great emblematical *Triad* of *Deity*, as with us they refer to the three principal officers of the Lodge. In the British Mysteries the *Adytum* or lodge was *actually* supported by three stones or pillars, which were supposed to convey a regenerating purity to the aspirant, after having endured the ceremony of initiation in all its accustomed formalities. The delivery from between them was termed a *new* birth.

309. "The Persians, who termed their emblematical mithratic cave or lodge the Empyrean, feigned to be supported by three intelligencies,—Ormisda, Mithra and Mithras; who were usually denominated, from certain characteristics which they were supposed individually to possess, *Eternity, Fecundity* and *Authority.*

310. "Similar to this were the forms of the Egyptian Deity, designed by the attributes of *Wisdom, Power* and *Goodness;* and the *Sovereign Good, Intellect* and *Energy* of the Platonists, which were also regarded as the respective properties of the Divine Triad.

311. "It is remarkable that every Mysterious system practiced on the habitable globe contained this Triad of Deity, which some writers refer to the Trinity, others to the triple offspring of Noah, and others to the three sons of Adam—Abel, Cain and Seth. The oracle in Damascus asserted that 'Throughout the world *A Triad shines forth, which resolves*

itself into a Monad,' and the uniform symbol of this three-fold Deity was an equilateral triangle, the precise form occupied by our pillars of Wisdom, Strength and Beauty.''*

312. ''The three Principal Officers of a lodge are, it is needless to say, situated in the East, West and South. Now, bearing in mind that the lodge is a symbol of the world, or the Universe, the reference of these three officers to the Sun at its rising, its setting, and its meridian height, must at once suggest itself.

313. ''In the Brahminical initiations of Hindustan, which are among the earliest that have been transmitted to us, and may almost be considered as the cradle of all the others of subsequent ages and various countries, the ceremonies were performed in vast caverns, the remains of some, of which, at Salsette, Elephanta, and a few other places, will give the spectator but a very inadequate idea of the extent and splendor of these Ancient Indian lodges.

314. ''The interior of the cavern of initiation was lighted by innumerable lamps, and there sat in the East, the West, and the South the principal Hierophants, or explainers of the Mysteries, as the representatives of Brahma, Vishnu, and Siva. Now, Brahma was the supreme Deity of the Hindoos, borrowed or derived from the Sun-god of their Sabean ancestors, and Vishnu and Siva were but manifestations of his attributes. We learn from the Indian Pantheon that 'when the sun rises in the east, he is

*Pierson, ''Traditions of Freemasonry.''

Brahma; when he gains his meridian in the south, he is Silva; and when he sets in the west, he is Vishnu."

315. "Again, in the Zoroasteric Mysteries of Persia, the temple of initiation was circular, being made so as to represent the Universe: the sun in the east, with the surrounding zodiac, formed an indispensable part of the ceremony of the reception.

316. "In the Egyptian Mysteries of Osiris, the same reference to the sun is contained, and Herodotus, who was himself an initiate, intimates that the ceremonies consisted in the representation of a Sun-god, who had been incarnate, that is, had *appeared on earth,* or rose, and *who was at length put to death* by Typhon, the symbol of darkness, typical of the sun's setting.

317. "In the great Mysteries of Eleusis, which were celebrated at Athens, we learn from St. Chrysostom, as well as other authorities, that the temple of initiation was *symbolic of the Universe,* and we *know* that one of the officers represented the sun."*

318. "In the East, as the pillar of Wisdom, this Deity was called Brahma; in the West, as the pillar of Strength, Vishnu; and in the South, as the pillar of Beauty, Siva, and hence, in the Indian initiations the representative of Brahma was seated in the East, that of Vishnu in the West and that of Siva in the South. A very remarkable coincidence with the practice of Ancient Masonry."**

*Mackey, "Symbolism of Freemasonry."
**Pierson, "Traditions of Freemasonry."

319. "The lodge continues throughout 'the degree to be presented to the initiated as a symbol of the world, and hence its covering is figuratively supposed to be the 'clouded canopy,' on which the host of stars is represented. The Mystical ladder which is here referred to as a symbol that was widely diffused among the religions of antiquity, where, as in Masonry, it was always supposed to consist of seven steps, because *seven was a Sacred number*. In some of the Ancient Mysteries the seven steps represented the seven planets and the Sun was the top-most."*

320. "The lodge as a representation of the world, is, of course, supposed to have no other roof than the heavens; and it would scarcely be necessary to enter into any discussion on the subject, were it not that another symbol—the theological ladder—is so intimately connected with it, that the one naturally suggests the other. Now, this Mystic ladder, which connects the ground floor of the lodge with its roof or covering, is another important and interesting link, which binds, with one common chain, the symbolism and rites of the Ancient Initiation.

321. "This Mystical ladder, which in Masonry is referred to as 'the theological ladder, which Jacob in his vision saw, reaching from earth to heaven,' was widely dispersed among the religions of antiquity, where it was always supposed to consist of seven rounds or steps.

---

*Mackey, "Manual of the Lodge."

322. "There is an anomaly in giving to the Mystical ladder of Masonry only *three* rounds. It is an anomaly, however, with which Masonry has had nothing to do. The error arose from the ignorance of those inventors who first engraved the Masonic symbols for our monitors. The ladder of Masonry, like the equipollent ladders of its kindred institutions, always had seven steps, although in modern times the three principal or upper ones are alone alluded to. These rounds, beginning at the lowest, are *Temperance, Fortitude, Prudence, Justice, Faith, Hope and Charity. Charity,* therefore, *takes the same place in the ladder of Masonic virtues as the sun does in the ladder or planets.*

323. "If Charity is equivalent to Divine Love, and Divine Love is represented by the sun, and lastly, if Charity be the topmost round of the Masonic ladder, then again we arrive, as the result of our researches, at the symbol so often already repeated of the solar orb. The natural sun or the Spiritual Sun—the sun, either as the vivifying principle of animated nature, and therefore the special object of adoration, or as the most prominent instrument of the Creator's benevolence—was ever a leading idea in the symbolism of antiquity."*

324. "There is a tradition of St. John the Baptist which has collateral evidence to sustain it. His father and mother died during his minority, and he was adopted by the Essenes, living with them in the

---

*Mackey, "Symbolism of Freemasonry."

wilderness, and when of proper age he was initiated in their Mysteries* and finally arrived to the chief dignity of the order. His diet and manner of living were perfectly conformable to the rules of the Essenes. They lived in the country; so did he. They dwelt near the river Jordan and baptized their disciples; John did the same, and thus acquired the cognomen of the Baptist. The Essenes fed on dates and other fruits,** and in many other respects agreed with the character of John, as we find him in the gospels.

325. "The fact that each, St. John the Baptist and St. John the Evangelist, were Eminent Essenes, is a sufficient reason why, in later times, Masons should dedicate their lodges to them without looking for or assigning any others, although doubtless our ancient brethren had other reasons.

326. "Masonic Monitors say: 'And since their time (St. John the Baptist and St. John the Evangelist), there is represented in every regular and well-governed Lodge a certain point within a circle, embordered by two perpendicular parallel lines, representing St. John the Baptist and St. John the Evangelist, and upon the top rests the Holy Scripture.' "*

327 "The two parallel lines which in the modern lectures are said to represent St. John the Baptist and St. John the Evangelist, really allude to particular periods in the sun's annual course. At two particular points in this course the Sun is found on the Zodiacal

* **See the "Philosophy of Fire" Chapter on the Essenian Initiation.

*Pierson, "Traditions of Freemasonry."

11

signs, Cancer and Capricorn, which are distinguished as the summer and winter solstices. When the sun is in these points, he has reached his greatest northern and southern limits. These points, if we suppose the circle to represent the sun's annual course, will be indicated by the points where the parallel lines touch the circle.''*

328. ''The mysteries among the Chinese and Japanese came from India and had similar rites. The Equilaterial triangle was one of their symbols, and so was the mystical Y; both alluding to the Triune God and the latter being the ineffable name of Deity, and for which symbol the modern Masons have substituted the Forty-seventh Problem of Euclid from its similarity in shape, having lost the explanation of their original symbol. A ring supported by two serpents was emblematical of the world protected by the power and wisdom of the Creator; and that is the origin of the two parallel lines (into which time has changed the two serpents) that support the circle in our lodges.

329. ''In the Druidical Rites the point within the circle and the cube were emblems of Odin, the Supreme God, the author of everything that existed, the Eternal, the Ancient and Living and Awful Being, the searcher into concealed things, the being that never changeth.

330. ''The point within became a universal emblem to denote the temple of the Deity, and was referred to the planetary circle in the *center* of which was fixed

*Mackey, ''Manual of the Lodge.''

the sun, as the universal god and father of nature; for the whole circle of heaven was called God. It was believed that the *center* of a temple was the peculiar residence of the Deity; the exterior decorations being merely ornamental. Mexico, Britain, Egypt, India, etc., present us many remains of temples built in circular form, in the center of which still remains the point or emblems of Divinity.

331. "All nations recognized as an object of worship a great Supreme Deity by whom all that was, was made. Another idea was that nothing possessing life could be created without the junction of the active and passive generative powers. And as God created all life, he must necessarily possess *within* himself each of those powers, and hence the Phallic worship, so common among the ancient nations, the symbol of which was the emblem that we have been considering, and which is found in this connection in the monuments of antiquity everywhere."*

332. "The Point within a Circle is derived from the Ancient Sun worship, and is in reality of Phallic origin. It is a symbol of the Universe, the Sun being represented by the point, while the circumference is the Universe."**

333. "The point within a circle is an interesting and important symbol in Freemasonry, but it has been so debased in the interpretation of it in the modern lectures that the sooner that interpretation is

*Pierson, "Traditions of Freemasonry."
**Mackey, "Symbolism of Freemasonry."

forgotten by the Masonic student, the better will it be. The symbol is really a beautiful but somewhat abstruse allusion to the old Sun-Worship, and introduces us for the first time to that modification of it, known among the ancients as the worship of the Phallus.''*

334. ''Perfectly to understand this symbol, I must refer, as a preliminary matter, to the worship of the Phallus, a peculiar modification of sun-worship, which prevailed to a great extent among the nations of antiquity.

335. ''The Phallus was a sculptured representation of the *Membrum Virile,* or male organ of generation, and the worship of it is said to have originated in Egypt, where, after the murder of Osiris by Typhon, which is symbolically to be explained as the destruction or deprivation of the sun's light by night, Isis, his wife, or the symbol of nature, in the search for his mutilated body, is said to have found all the parts except the organs of generation, which myth is simply symbolic of the fact, that the sun having set, its fecundating and invigorating power had ceased. The Phallus, therefore, as the symbol of the male generative principle, was very universally venerated among the ancients, and that, too, as a religious rite, without *the slightest reference to any impure or lascivious application.* He is supposed, by some commentators, to be the god mentioned under the name of Baal-peor, in the Book of Numbers, as having been worshipped by the idolatrous Moabites. Among the Eastern nations

*Mackey, ''Manual of the Lodge.''

of India the same symbol was prevalent, under the name of 'Lingam.' But the Phallus or Lingam was a representation of the male principle only. To perfect the circle of generation it is necessary to advance one step farther. Accordingly we find in the *Cteis* of the Greeks, and the *Yoni* of the Indians, a symbol of the female generative principle, or co-extensive prevalence with the Phallus. The *Cteis* was a circular and conclave pedestal or receptacle, on which the Phallus or column rested, and from the center of which it sprang.

336. "The union of the Phallus and Cteis, or the Lingam and Yoni, in one compound figure, as an object of adoration, was the most usual mode of representation. This was in strict accordance with the whole system of Ancient Mythology, which was founded upon a worship of the prolific powers of nature. All the Deities of pagan antiquity, however numerous they may be, can always be reduced to the two different forms of the generative principle—the active, or male, and the passive, or female. Hence the gods were always arranged in pairs, as Jupiter and Juno, Bacchus and Venus, Osiris and Isis,

Christ and *Mary.*

337. But the ancients went farther. Believing that the procreative and productive powers of nature might be conceived to exist in the same individual, they made the older of their Deities hermaphrodite, and used the term *man-virgin*, to denote the union of the two sexes in the same Divine person.

11a

338. "Now, this hermaphrodism of the Supreme Divinity was again supposed to be represented by the sun, which was the male generative energy, and by nature, or the universe, which was the female prolific principle. And this union was symbolized in different ways, but principally by *the point within the circle,* the point indicating the sun, and the circle the Universe, invigorated and fertilized by his generative rays.

339. "So far, then, we arrive at the true interpretation of the Masonic symbolism of the point within the circle. It is the same thing, but under different form, as the Master and Wardens of a lodge. The Master and Wardens are symbols of the sun, the lodge of the Universe, or world, just as the point is the symbol of the same sun, and the surrounding circle of the universe.

340. "But the two perpendicular parallel lines remain to be explained. Every one is familiar with the very recent interpretation, that they represent the two Saints John, the Baptist and the Evangelist. But this modern exposition must be abandoned, if we desire to obtain the true ancient signification."*

341. "A New Zealand myth says we have two primeval ancestors, a father and a mother. They are Rangi and Papa, heaven and earth. The earth, out of which all things are produced, is our mother; the protecting and over-ruling heaven is our father.

*Mackey, "Symbolism of Freemasonry."

342. "It is thus evident that the doctrine of the reciprocal principles of nature, or nature active and passive, male and female, was recognized in nearly all the primitive religious systems of the old as well as of the new world; and none more clearly than in those of Central America, thus proving not only the wide extent of the doctrine, but also a separate and independent origin, springing from those innate principles which are common to human nature in all climes and races. Hence the almost universal reverence paid to the images of the sexual parts, as they were regarded as symbols and types of the generative and productive principles in nature, and of those gods and goddesses who were the representatives of the same principles. 'The first doctrine to be taught men would have relation to their being. The existence of a creator could be illustrated by a potter at the wheel. But there was a much more expressive form familiar to them, indicative of cause and effect in the production of births in the tribe, or in nature. In this way the *Phallus* became the exponent of creative power; and, *though to our eyes vulgar and indecent, bore no improper meaning to the simple Ancient Worshipper.*' Bonwick, *Egyptian Belief*, p. 257. The Phallus and the Kteis, the Lingam and the Yoni—the special parts contributing to generation and production—becoming thus symbols of those active and passive causes, could not fail to become objects of reverence and worship. The union of the two symbolized the creative energy of all nature; for almost all primitive religion consisted in the reverence and worship paid to nature and

its operation.

343. "In those early ·days, all the operations of·
nature were consecrated to some divinity from whom
they were supposed to emanate; thus sowing of¯ the
seed was presided over by Ceres. 'Hevia,' writes
General Forlong, 'is equivalent to Zoe life, from the
Greek to live; thus what is called "the fall," ascribed
to Eva, or Hevia, the female, and Adam, the male, becomes in reality the acts connected with generation,
conception, and. production, and the destruction of
virginity.—Adam "fell" from listening to Eve, and
she from . the serpent tempting her,—details which
merely assure us that we have procreative acts in all
stories regarding Hawa (in Hindustani Lust, Wind,
Air-Juno) and Chavah or Eve, or as the Arabs call it,
Hayyat, life or creation. Eating forbidden fruit was
simply a *figurative* mode of expressing the performance of the act necessary for the perpetuation of
the human race.'

344. "This sacred festival does ·not astonish me,"
said Dr. Goodman. ·"I feel persuaded that· this was
·the first festival that men celebrated, and I do not· see
why we should not pray to God when we are going to
pro-create a being in His image, as we pray before we
take our food, which· serves to support our body;
··working to give birth to a reasonable being, is a most
noble and Holy action; as thus the first Indians
thought who revered the Lingam, the symbol of
generation; the ancient Egyptians who carried the
Phallus in procession; the Greeks who erected temples
to Priapus."

345. "The reverence as well as worship paid to the Phallus, in early primitive days, *had nothing in it which partook of indecency; all ideas connected with it were of a reverential and religious kind.* When Abraham, as mentioned in Genesis, in asking his servant to take a solemn oath, makes him lay his hand on his parts of generation (in the common version 'under his thigh'), it was that he required, as a token of his sincerity, his placing his hand on the most revered part of his body; as at the present day a man would place his hand on his heart in order to evince his sincerity. Jacob, when dying, makes his son Joseph perform the same act. A similar custom is still retained among the Arabs at the present day. An Arab, in taking a solemn oath, will place his hand on his virile member, in attestation of sincerity.

346. "The indecent ideas attached to the representation of the Phalus were, though it seems a paradox to say so, *the result of a more advanced civilization verging towards its decline,* as we have evidence at Rome and Pompeii.

347. "Our ideas of propriety lead us to suppose that a ceremony which appears to us infamous could only be invented by licentiousness; but it is impossible to believe that licentiousness and depravity of manners would ever have led among any people to the establishment of religious ceremonies, profligacy may have crept in in the lapse of time. *But the original institution was always innocent and free from it;* the *early agapes,* in which boys and girls kissed one

another modestly on the mouth, degenerated at last into secret meetings and licentiousness. It is, therefore, probable that this custom was first introduced in times of simplicity, that the first thought was to honor the Deity in the symbol of life which it has given us.''

348. ''To sum up, the Phallus, in the same manner as statues, plants, animals, objects of worship among nations, *was only the outward covering, the receptacle, the vehicle of the Deity which was supposed to be contained within it, a Deity to which alone Religious Worship was paid.* This outward covering, this receptacle, this vehicle, was varied in an infinity of modes with regard to its form, *but it was neither a symbol nor an allegory.''*

349. The Mysteries formed an important feature in the system of religion practiced amongst the Greeks. In the institutions of polytheism the gods were worshipped openly by prayer and sacrifice; and to these rites the people of every rank were admitted without distinction, because they formed the beaten track of duty which mortal man was supposed to owe to the immortal Deities. But the highest ceremonies of religion were of a nature *too sublime to be exposed to public-view;* and were, therefore, only celebrated in the presence of that distinguished portion of the community which had bound themselves by voluntary vows to preserve the solemn rites inviolably secret from the rest of the world.

350. ''These Rites were known under the high and

*Hodder M. Westropp, ''Primitive symbolism.''

significant appellation of The Mysteries; and even in them a subdivision had been made, because it was thought dangerous to entrust the ineffable secrets to any but a select and chosen few, *who are prepared to a new accession of knowledge by processes, at once seductive and austere, and bound to secrecy by fearful oaths, and penalties of the most sanguinary.* The former were denominated *the lesser,* and these *the greater Mysteries.*"*

351. Among the Ancients Silence and Secrecy were considered virtues of the highest order. The Egyptians worshipped Harpocrates, the God of Secrecy, raised altars in his name, and wreathed them with garlands of flowers. Among the ancient Romans, too, these virtues were not less esteemed, and a distinguished Latin poet tells us, "For faithful Silence also there is a sure reward."

352. It must not be supposed that any of the Ancient Initiates really worshipped the god of secrecy, but like in all else, they worshipped that which this god Harpocrates represented. The one thing in which Historians make their great and inexplicable mistake is to take the symbol for the actual fact or *idea.* Few races, even among the heathens, have worshipped idols but *that which these idols represent.* In this is the secret and solution of all Ancient Religion as well as in modern Freemasonry.

353. "We find among all the priests of ancient people, and in order that none but really capable and

---

*Oliver, "History of Initiation."

worthy men should be associated with their offices and studies, they instituted forms of probation and examination upon which followed some kind of initiation. Now as the oldest writers ascribe such mysteries and initiations to the Egyptian Priests, it is very probable that they already existed before the downfall of that people, for we find traces of them in equally ancient nations and perceive from the likeness of their fundamental principles and of the teachings and customs of their priests, that they must have had a common origin and *that origin was on the lost Atlantis.* Among the Chaldeans and Magi dwelt on the summits of the mountains, and among the Celtic races the Druids lived in the quiet solitude of the forests. Among the Indians and Ethiopians the Brahmins and Gymnosophists had localities specially dedicated to them, and among the Egyptians the Priests had intricate dwelling-places far beneath the surface of the earth. All had their symbols and distinctive signs, and owed their fame only to the Secrecy of their Initiation.

354. "The Secrets of Antiquity had a two-fold aim. In the first case Religion was chosen as the object of care; the Greater the Mysteries the more eternally secret were they to be kept from the people. The aim in the second case was to guard the Wisdom of all things. He who would be initiated must be a man of upright character and true mental power. The Sacred Mysteries fell into decay with the Roman Empire, the flourishing and spread of the Christian

religion being the chief cause of this decadence. The initiation into the Mysteries of the Wisdom was, however, of much longer duration. They changed only from time to time either the name, the inner constitution, the degrees and various kinds of knowledge bound up in these, or even the nature of the union itself. The men, who were known under the name of Magi, or the White Masters, made one of their most important aims the true knowledge of the human heart, which lay always open before their eyes.

355. To them alone was entrusted the bringing up of Kings and the great on earth, for they alone could understand science as well as art, and careless of all prejudice taught a *simple* and *natural* Theology, which based itself upon the worship of a Supreme Being.

356. Because, however, their method of teaching was symbolical, many errors of *which they were entirely incapable* were ascribed to them on account of their numerous hieroglyphics. The Magi of Memphis and Heliopolis were held in such esteem, and their renown was so widespread that the greatest heroes of war, philosophers, and strangers of the highest rank journeyed to Egypt and sought to be initiated by the Priests in order to learn the secrets of the Priesthood. From among these priests Lycurgus and Solon drew a part of their system of Philosophy; and Orpheus was also initiated by them, and by this means enabled to introduce into his own land, festivals from which the Greek mythology afterwards arose. Thales also was instructed by them, Pythagoras received from the

same source his doctrine of Metempsychosis, Herodotus obtained much information, and Democritus his secrets. Moses also, who was brought up by the Magi, used his knowledge of the Mysteries to free the Israelites from Egyptian bondage and lead them to the service of the *true* God. It is well known that Moses prescribed certain probation for his Levites, and that the secrets of the Priesthood were inaccessible to the rest of the Israelites, and this principle rules till the time of Solomon.

357. This policy of Silence and Secrecy has *always* been a wise one, for the bitter vituperations which have nearly always been showered on the heads of those who were the Exoteric leaders in such Orders, has demonstrated the wisdom which guarded the personalities of the real leaders. Thus the same system of Secrecy is still followed.

RULES and REGULATIONS

GOVERNING THE MEMBERS OF THE

ANCIENT and MYSTICAL ORIENTAL RITE

Adopted in Secret Council held in in the East
In the year of Our Lord 1906.

Rules are ABSOLUTELY binding on all Lodges and its members under the Supreme Grand Lodge jurisdiction.

RULES

---

1. The whole world is but one Republic, of which each Nation is a family, and every individual a child. Masonry, and especially Mystic Masonry, not in anywise derogating from the differing duties which the diversity of States requires, tends to create a new people, a new association, a Universal Brotherhood, which, composed of men of many nations and tongues, shall all be bound together by the bonds of Science, Morality, Virtue and Brotherly Love.

2. The real object of Mystic Masonry can be summed up in these words: To efface from among men the prejudice of caste, the conventional distinctions of color, origin, opinion, nationality; to annihilate fanaticism and superstition, extirpate national discord and with it extinguish the firebrand of war; in a word —to arrive, by free and pacific progress, at one formula or model of eternal and universal right, according to which each individual human being shall be

free to develop every faculty with which he may be
endowed, and to concur heartily and with all the
fullness of his strength, in the bestowment of happiness upon all, and thus to make of the whole human
race one family of brothers, united by affection,
wisdom and labor and to bind them together in such a
way *that it shall be impossible for one brother to hurt
another in any possible way.*

3. Masonic Charity and devotion being the duty of
brothers, whosoever shall be convicted of having had
projects or acts tending to lower the Order, or attack
a brother's honor, shall, by the very deed, be brought
before the Committee appointed in such cases and if
found guilty, shall not only be expelled, but shall be
made to suffer the full penalty of such act as is prescribed by the *Secret Code.* There can be no excep-
tions to these rules and laws, for to do so were to
weaken the very foundation of Mystic and Oriental
Masonry.

4. When the calamities of a brother call for our aid,
we should not withdraw the hand that might sustain
him from sinking but we *must* render him those
services, which, not incumbering or injuring our
families or fortunes, charity and religion may dictate
for the saving of our fellow being, nor may we draw

the line too closely in our own favor. Mystic Masonry, if for anything, is to bind its members together in one bond which *cannot* be severed by any force whatever.

5. From this purpose, indolence dare *not* persuade the foot to halt or wrath turn our steps out of the way; but forgetting injuries and selfish feelings, and remembering that man was born for the aid of his generation and not for his own enjoyment only, but to do that which is good, we *must* be swift to have mercy, to save, to strengthen and execute benevolence.

6. As the good things of this life are partially dispensed, and some are opulent, while others are in distress, such principles also enjoin Mystic Masons, even if ever so poor, to testify their good will towards each other. Riches alone do not allow the means of doing good; *virtue and benevolence* are not confined to the walks of opulence; the rich man, from his many talents, is required to make extensive works under the principles of virtue, and yet poverty is no excuse for an omission of that exercise; for as the cry of innocence ascendeth up to heaven, as the voice of babes and sucklings reach the throne of God, and as the breathings of a contrite heart are heard in the regions of dominion, so a Mystic's prayers, devoted to the welfare of his brother, are required of him.

12a

7. Another principle is *never* to injure the confidence of your brother by revealing his secrets; for perhaps, that were to rob him of the guard which protects his property or life. The tongue of a Mystic Mason *must* be void of offense and without guile towards a brother, speaking truth with discretion and keeping itself within the rule of judgment, maintaining a heart void of uncharitableness, locking up secrets and communing in charity and love.

8. So much is required of the Mystic Mason in his gifts as discretion shall limit; charity begins at home, but like a fruitful olive tree planted by the side of a fountain whose boughs overshoot the wall, so is charity; it spreads its arms abroad from the strength and opulence of its station and bendeth its shade for the repose and relief of those who are gathered under its branches. Charity, when given with imprudence, is no longer a virtue; but when flowing from abundance, it is glorious as the beams of morning, in whose beauty thousands rejoice. When, donations, extorted by pity, are detrimental to a man's family, they become sacrifices to superstition, and like incense to idols are disapproved by heaven.

9. In the intercourse with the world, we must carefully guard ourselves against depreciating any brother

of the Order, *no matter what his faults may be.* We must *not* let any words of ill-will fall from our lips relating to the members of our Fraternity. If, from motives of jealousy at our success and progress, they choose to be antagonistic to us, let all the aggressive acts be on the other side; for if Mystic Masons disagree among themselves, and make their dissensions matters of public notoriety, what opinion of us can we expect from the outer world, and how can it believe in our profession of Brotherly Love, Friendship and the Universal Brotherhood of Man?

10. As the Ancient Mystic Oriental Masons of the Universe consider the Blue Lodge or Ancient Craft Masonry the foundation and fundamental basis of our Institution, to which the Masonic allegiance of all its members is due, and from which there can be no deviation; therefore, no Mason can be allowed to join the Ancient Mystic Oriental Rite of the Universe unless he is a member of some Ancient Free and Accepted Masonic Body.

11. Initiates of Mystic and Oriental Masonry are ordered to fraternize with the members of all other Rites. "Tolerance" is not only written at the head of all its Sacred Laws, but is an *absolute and unbreakable* rule. There is but one exception to this rule.

No Mystic Mason can, under any circumstances, recognize the member of any Masonic Body in which the "G" does not hold a prominent place. In such cases Masonic rule is broken and in this respect Albert G. Mackey, the Highest Masonic authority on the Continent of America, in his Masonic Jurisprudence, says: "Within the past few years an attempt has been made by some Grand Lodges to add to these simple, moral, and religious qualifications, another, which requires a belief in the Divine authenticity of the Scriptures. It is much to be regretted that Masons will sometimes forget the *fundamental law of their Institution, and endeavor to add to or to detract from the perfect integrity of the building, as it was left to them by their predecessors.* Whenever this is done, the beauty of our temple must suffer. "The Landmarks of Masonry are so perfect that they neither need nor will permit of the slightest amendment."

12. The "G" in the Masonic Institution is the oldest Landmark the institution has and to take this away is to break Masonic Rule. It is un-Masonic and any Grand Lodge doing this is not only un-Masonic but becomes, by that very act, Spurious or Clandestine Masonry. *This is Masonic Law.* It cannot be broken.*

*"G" This letter is *deservedly* regarded as one of the MOST *sacred* of the Masonic emblems. Where it is

13. It is an absolute rule that the Ritual *must* be used in all Initiation work. This is nothing new even among Craft Masonry. Says a member of the Belgium Lodge: "Our Lodge, called 'La Charite,' at Orient Charlevoi, is under obedience of the great Orient at Brussels, and has the Scottish Rite. No Mason is supposed to know anything of the ritual by heart. Questions and answers are read out, especially at initiation. *The work of the Mason is supposed to be interior work in himself, before it can become exterior labor.* So in order to obtain his degrees he has to do some work of his own, and no one is supposed to learn anything by heart, except words, signs and passwords. Now I have to tell you that every Mason is

---

used, however, as a symbol of Deity, it must be remembered that it is the Saxon representative of the Hebrew *Yod* and the Greek *Tau*—the initial letters of the name of the Eternal in those Languages. This symbol proves that Freemasonry always prosecuted its labors with reference to the grand ideas of Infinity and Eternity. By the letter "G"—which conveys to the minds of the brethren, at the same time, the idea of God and that of Geometry—*it bound heaven to earth, the Divine to the human, and the infinite to the finite.* Masons are taught to regard the Universe as the grandest of all symbols, revealing to men, in all ages, the ideas which are eternally revolving in the mind of the Divinity, and which it is their duty to reproduce in their own lives and in the world of art and industry.

supposed to do some literary work on general subjects concerning the welfare of man, human institutions, sociology, history, philosophy, philanthrophy, etc., and it is such work that a young Mason is supposed to do. Then, after reading these papers, they are discussed by all the members of the Lodge present, perhaps for three or four meetings, until the subject seems to be exhausted. This develops, in the young Mason, his intelligence and his moral feeling." According to this it is not forbidden in Craft Masonry to use the Rituals during labor and the Supreme Lodge of Ancient and Oriental Mystic Masonry now makes it an absolute rule that All Lodges *must* use the Ritual during labor. There can be no exception to this rule. To dis-

---

Thus God and Geometry, the material worlds and the Spiritual spheres, were constantly united in the speculations of the ancient Masons. They, consequently, labored earnestly and unweariedly, not only to construct cities, and embellish them with magnificent edificies, *but also to built up a temple of great and Divine thoughts and of ever-growing virtues for the Soul to dwell in.** The symbolical letter "G"—

—————————'That hieroglyphic bright, Which none but craftsmen ever saw,"

and before which every *true* Mason reverently uncovers, and bows his head—is a perpetual condemnation of pro-

*The true meaning of the Temple of Sol-om-on, called Solomon's Temple.

obey means the revocation of the Charter of such Lodge.

14. Whosoever wishes to be admitted to the secrets, and afterwards to be initiated, must be a man of honor and of true spiritual power; he must already be of some learning in the Mysteries concerning initiation; for only those will be accepted who will be of service to the great work. It will be necessary that he shall be a member of the M........ C........ E........ have taken the Obligation as a Brother and have his name enrolled among that Order. After this is done he can make application for Initiation into the Lodge.

15. The Supreme Grand Master, or his Deputy, has Authority and Right, not only to be present in any

---

fanity, impiety and vice. No brother who has bowed before that emblem can be profane. He will never speak the name of the Grand Master of the Universe but with reverence, respect and—*Love*. He will learn, by studing the Mystic meaning of the letter "G", to model his life after the Divine plan ; and, thus instructed, he will strive to be like God in the activity and earnestness of his benevolence, and the broadness and efficiency of his charity. "The letter "G" occupies a prominent position in several of the degrees in the American system ; is found in many of the degrees of the Ancient and Accepted Scottish rite ; in Adonhiramite Masonry ; and, in fact, in every one of the

true Lodge, but also to preside wherever he is, with the Master of the Lodge on his left hand, and to order the other Officers to do such duty as he may wish.

16. The Master of a particular Lodge has the Right and Authority of congregating the Members of his Lodge into a Chapter at pleasure, upon any Emergency or Occurrence, as well as to appoint the time and place of their usual meeting. In case of the sickness of the Master no Lodge can be opened. In the case of the death of the Master of any of the other Officers, the Deputy Grand Master will appoint a successor.

17. The Master of each particular Lodge shall keep

---

many systems in which the people of the sixteenth and seventeenth century were so prolific in manufacturing. Wherever we find this recondite symbol in any of the Masonic rites, it has the same significance —a substitute for the Hebraic *jod*, the initial letter of the Divine name, and a monogram that expressed the Uncreated Being, Principal of ALL things; and inclosed in a Triangle, the unity of God. We recognize the same letter "G" in the Syriac *Gad*, the Swedish *Gud*, the German *Gutt*, and the English *God*--all names of the Deity and all derived from the Persian *Goda*, itself derived from the absolute pronoun signifying *himself*."*

*Macoy and Oliver "History and Cyclopedia of Freemasonry."

a Book containing their By-laws, the Names of their Members, with a list of other Lodges in such state or country. A copy of the Secret Laws shall also be kept in such Lodge and each member must possess a copy of such Secret Laws.

18. No man can be made or admitted a member of a particular Lodge, without previous notice one Month before given to the said Lodge, in order to make due inquiry into the reputation and capacity of the Candidate; unless by Special Dispensation. No man can be admitted or made unless he first becomes a member of the ....

19. "The candidate shall solemnly promise to submit to the Constitutions, the Charges, Regulations, and such other Usages as shall be intimated to him in time and place convenient.

20. No set or number of Brethren shall withdraw or separate themselves from the Lodge in which they were made Brethren, or were afterwards admitted Members, unless the Lodge becomes too numerous; nor even then, without a Dispensation from the Supreme Grand Master; and when they are thus separated, they must either immediately join themselves to such other Lodge as they shall be ordered, or else

they must obtain the Supreme Grand Master's warrant to join in forming a new Lodge.

21. If any number of Brethren shall take upon
themselves to form a Lodge without the Supreme,
Grand Master's Warrant, the regular Lodges are not
to countenance them, nor own them as fair Brethren
and duly formed, but treat them as Rebels. It will
be impossible that this should happen for the reason
that the Brethren can only reach the Supreme Grand
Master through the Deputy and since not even the
Masters of the Lodges can come into direct contact
with the *unknown* Supreme Grand Master, and since
no one but the candidate for the Highest Degrees can
know the Supreme Grand Master, it will be impossible to form such clandestine Lodges, since their very
support and source of Light would be totally cut off
from them. Besides this, The *Secret Code* absolutely
forbids this and under the Obligation that each
Brother takes before he can be admitted to even the
first degree of Mystic Masonry, he can never betray
either a Brother or the Lodge to which he belongs,
much less the Supreme Grand Lodge.

22. If any Brother so far misbehaves himself as to
render his Lodge uneasy, he shall be admonished by
the Master in the formed Lodge; and if he will not

refrain his Imprudence, and obediently submit to the advice of the Brethren, and reform what gives them Offense, he shall be dealt with according to the Secret Rules, for the Lodge of Mystic Masonry combines both the Church and the Academy and the Brethren meet for instruction and worship, therefore, no inharmony can be allowed to prevail.

23. All Lodges are to observe the same Usages as much as possible, in order to do this, and for cultivating a good understanding among Mystic Masons, some members out of every Lodge shall be deputed to visit other Lodges as often as shall be thought convenient and each Lodge, or several may combine, may form a College for secret instruction of its members.

27. The Supreme Grand Lodge consists of the *unknown* Supreme Grand Master, the Supreme Grand Master, the Supreme Grand Deputy, the Grand Secretary, the Grand Deputies of the States and the Secret Teacher or Hierophants of the Higher Degrees. The Brethren who come into touch with the Hierophants are absolutely forbidden, as per their Obligation, to ever reveal the abiding place of any Hierophant.

25. The Supreme Grand Master holds such position for life and selects his own Deputy, Secretary,

Deputies and other Officers. He may resign and appoint his successor and each new Supreme Grand Master has the authority to formulate his own Rules and Regulations with the exception of the Secret Rules. He can choose his own Seal and even change the name of the Order. He must, however, retain all Deputies who have proven proficient under former Supreme Grand Masters and he cannot, under any circumstances, change the Grand Hierophants. He cannot change any of the degrees nor any of the Lodges. Each Supreme Grand Master must select his successor immediately after he takes charge of his office and such a one as he selects must be under his instructions for no less than ten years, unless, as it sometimes happens, that the Supreme Grand Master meets with an untimely death. The one who then succeeds him in office cannot, under his Obligation, cause any inharmony in the Order.

26. The Supreme Grand Master issues all Dispensations and Warrants for Lodges throughout the known world. He shall keep a book, or appoint a Secretary to keep such book, wherein be recorded all the Lodges, with their usual times and places of meeting, and the names of all the members of each Lodge; and all the affairs of the Supreme Grand Lodge that are

proper to be written. Such books must be kept in the Secret Archives of the Order, together with all such other Secret Manuscripts and documents as may come into the possession of the Supreme Grand Body.

27. The Supreme Grand Master *cannot* abuse his power, even with his almost unlimited authority for the reason that the Grand Hierophants and the Great White Brotherhood are above him in authority and he is always held accountable to them for anything that he may do.

FOR SALE BY

Purdy Publishing Co.

40 RANDOLPH ST.

CHICAGO, ILL.

Milton Keynes UK
Ingram Content Group UK Ltd.
UKHW051337140124
436020UK00002B/5